Vegetarian Cookbook for Beginners

Vegetarian Cookbook
for Beginners

The Essential Vegetarian Cookbook to Get Started

ROCKRIDGE
PRESS

Photography © Jennifer Davick 2015, cover; Marti Sans/Stocksy, p. 2; Alessio Bogani/Stocksy, p. 6; Kristin Duvall/Stocksy, pp. 10, 58, 88, 216 & back cover; Greg Schmigel/Stocksy, p. 18; Marilar Irastorza/Stocksy, pp. 26, 180 & back cover; Paul Edmondson/Stocksy, pp. 34 & 136; Suzanne Clements/Stocksy, pp. 44 & 122; Alexander Grabchilev/Stocksy, p. 52; Nastasa Mandic/Stocksy, pp. 64 & back cover; Alberto Bogo/Stocksy, p. 156.

ISBN Print 978-1-62315-242-0 | eBook 978-1-62315-277-2

Contents

Introduction

When you think about food or see commercials for restaurants on TV, what are the things that catch your eye? Chances are good that your eye isn't drawn to that bowl of veggies sitting off to the side of a sizzling platter of chicken fajitas. We can't help it—we are drawn to food we know. Though meat is the focus of many modern Western diets, it shouldn't always be in the spotlight. Vegetable-based dishes can play more than just a supporting role—they can shine just as brightly (or more brightly) than any meat-based dish.

The vegetarian diet is based solely on vegetable-based foods. Some vegetarians choose to eat eggs, milk, and other dairy products, but most refrain from consuming any type of meat that comes from animals or fish. For those of us who live in a world where the local McDonald's gets more traffic than the local library or park, it can be difficult to imagine a diet that doesn't include meat. Set aside your doubts for a moment and picture this:

Thick slices of tender eggplant tossed in flour and fried to perfection, sandwiched between layers of fresh mozzarella and herbed tomato sauce—served hot on a bed of fresh linguine al dente and paired with a glass of merlot.

If that description doesn't get your mouth watering, nothing will. Vegetarian food does not have to be bland or boring just because it doesn't include meat; in fact, when you remove meat from the equation, you will be able to experience the unique flavors and textures that fruits and vegetables have to offer. After just a few weeks on the vegetarian diet, you will find that you do not miss meat at all. The thought of a crisp, refreshing salad or a hot bowl of vegetable stew will get your stomach growling more than a chicken breast or filet of beef ever could.

The vegetarian diet is about more than just eating good food, though that is certainly one of the rewards. For many people, it is about the myriad health benefits this type of diet has to offer. Countless studies have shown that those who do not eat meat often have lower blood cholesterol levels, reduced risk for chronic disease, improved insulin response, and lower body weight—not to mention an increased life span!

Do what is best for your body by switching to a vegetarian diet. In this book you will find all of the information you need to make the transformation. From explanations of what vegetarianism is, how it can benefit you, and how to make the transition to delicious recipes for snacks, entrées, and desserts, this book will serve as your guide on the path toward a healthy, meat-free lifestyle.

Part One

SALAD OVER STEAK

Understanding Vegetarianism

ONE

What Is Vegetarianism?

The term *vegetarianism* refers to the practice of abstaining from the consumption of meat and, in some cases, eggs and dairy products. The word *vegetarian* was first used by the Vegetarian Society, which was founded in 1847 in Manchester, England. The Vegetarian Society was established as a means of supporting and representing vegetarians in the United Kingdom in addition to spreading the word about the vegetarian lifestyle. Today, the Vegetarian Society continues to work for the support and education of vegetarians and other individuals, while also acting as a pressure group, aiming to influence food manufacturers to remove nonvegetarian additives from their food products.

A few notable vegetarians and members of the Vegetarian Society include the following:

- Alec Baldwin
- Bramwell Booth
- Cesar Chavez
- Jorja Fox
- Mahatma Gandhi
- Richard Gere
- Tony Gonzalez

- Coretta Scott King
- Dr. Anna Kingsford
- Paul McCartney
- Henry Salt
- Cicely Tyson
- Kate Winslet

Different Types of Vegetarianism

There are a number of different types of vegetarianism, based on the types of food an individual does and does not eat. While all types of vegetarianism are centered on a primarily fruit- and vegetable-based diet, certain types of vegetarianism exclude the consumption of eggs, milk, dairy, and/or animal products. The following chart provides a basic overview of the different types of vegetarianism:

Types of Vegetarianism

	FRUIT	VEG.	NUTS/ SEEDS	MEAT	FISH	EGGS	MILK	DAIRY	ANIMAL PRODUCTS
FLEXITARIAN	X	X	X	X*	X*	X	X	X	X
PESCATARIAN	X	X	X		X	X	X	X	X
LACTO-OVO-VEGETARIAN	X	X	X			X	X	X	X
OVO-VEGETARIAN	X	X	X			X			X
LACTO-VEGETARIAN	X	X	X				X	X	X
VEGAN	X	X	X						
RAW VEGAN	X	X	X						
FRUITARIAN	X		X						

* Eaten only on occasion (follows a mostly vegetarian diet).

PESCATARIAN

A pescatarian (also spelled pescetarian) abstains from all meat except for fish and seafood. This type of diet is often used as a stepping stone toward a full vegetarian diet.

FLEXITARIAN

Flexitarians are also referred to as semivegetarians because they follow a mostly vegetarian diet but sometimes consume meat or fish. In some cases, flexitarians define "meat" only as mammalian flesh, excluding fish and poultry from the definition.

LACTO-OVO-VEGETARIAN

Also called ovo-lacto-vegetarians, this group of vegetarians consumes eggs, milk, dairy, and other animal products, including honey.

OVO-VEGETARIAN

Ovo-vegetarians eat eggs in addition to fruits, vegetables, nuts, and seeds. They do not, however, consume milk or other dairy products.

LACTO-VEGETARIAN

This group, in addition to fruits, vegetables, nuts, and seeds, lacto-vegetarians also consume milk and dairy products. They do not, however, consume eggs.

VEGAN

Vegans take things one step further than traditional vegetarians by eliminating all animal products from their diets. This includes meat, eggs, milk, cheese, and other dairy products. Some vegans also choose not to use clothing or other products that are derived from animal sources; these may include honey, fur, leather, silk, wool, whey, lard, and beeswax. Strict vegans may also refrain from using cosmetics and other products that have been tested on animals.

RAW VEGAN

Raw vegans follow the same dietary guidelines as vegans, but they do not consume any food that has been heated above 115°F. This dietary practice is based on the idea that cooking foods above 115°F destroys the natural enzymes contained within the food and also results in a loss of nutritional value.

FRUITARIAN

Those following a fruitarian diet consume only fruit, nuts, and seeds. Other plant matter that can be gathered without killing or harming the plant may also be permitted; this includes foods that fall naturally from a plant such as fruits and seeds.

Why Do People Become Vegetarians?

The list of reasons why a person might switch to a vegetarian diet is long and varied. For many people, it is a matter of dietary preference or medical necessity as much as it is a matter of concern for the environment or for animal rights. You will find below an in-depth exploration of some of the most common reasons people make the switch to a vegetarian diet.

REASONS PEOPLE SWITCH TO A VEGETARIAN DIET INCLUDE:

- Medical reasons
- Ethical/political concerns
- Dietary preference
- Environmental concern
- Religious affiliation

Ethical/Political Concerns For many people, making the switch to a vegetarian diet is as much a means of opposing cruelty to animals as it is a means of opposition to the meat industry itself. More than 650,000 animals are killed per hour for meat in the United States, and total meat and poultry production in 2011 exceeded 92 billion pounds. Though there are about 60 major beef-packing plants nationwide, four companies control more than 80 percent of the U.S. beef industry.

Though supporters of the meat industry cite the statistic that the industry employs more than 6 million people and its revenue makes up about 6 percent of the entire country's GDP, the meat industry may not be as beneficial as it is cracked up to be. Slaughterhouse workers have the highest rate of occupational turnover in the United States, in addition to the highest rate of on-the-job injury. These facts suggest that not only is the meat industry harmful to animals, but it can also be very dangerous for humans.

Medical Reasons Next to ethical concerns, medical necessity is one of the most commonly cited motivations for switching to a vegetarian diet. Countless medical research studies have established a link between the modern Western diet and the proliferation of chronic diseases such as diabetes, cancer, and heart disease in Western cultures. It has been shown that overconsumption of meat and animal fat contributes to increased blood cholesterol levels, which not only affects heart health but can also lead to dangerous weight gain and central obesity. A vegetarian diet has been proven to not only reduce blood cholesterol levels and to help regulate blood sugar, but in many cases to entirely reverse the effects of several serious medical conditions. People who are not currently suffering from chronic disease may also make the switch to a vegetarian diet as a means of preventing these problems from developing.

Dietary Preference For many people, making the switch to a vegetarian diet is a means of dietary preference or food availability. Some people simply do not like the taste or texture of meat, while others are unable to afford the purchase of quality meat on a regular basis. In cases like these, becoming a vegetarian may not be so much a conscious choice as a result of preference or limited access to meat.

Environmental Concern People who switch to a vegetarian diet out of environmental concern typically believe that the rearing of livestock involves the inefficient use of crops and that it can also be damaging to the environment. Livestock production requires the use of valuable resources such as land, fossil fuels, and water. It may also contribute to air pollution, land degradation, deforestation, and a decline in biodiversity. For some people, going vegetarian is an ethical response to the livestock industry's abuse and exploitation of the environment.

Another issue connected to environmental concern and vegetarianism is sustainability. Rather than utilizing crops for human consumption, millions of tons of grain, corn, and soybeans are funneled through the industrial agriculture system each year. It takes about 7 pounds of grain to produce 1 pound of beef. The Worldwatch Institute suggests that the meat industry is the primary reason why millions of people around the globe are starving when there is more than enough food available to feed the entire planet. It also states that "meat consumption is an inefficient use of grain—continued growth in meat output is dependent on feeding grain to animals, creating competition for grain between affluent meat-eaters and the world's poor."

Religious Affiliation Several of the world's most common religions advocate for healthy eating, and both Hinduism and Buddhism advocate for vegetarianism specifically. People who are Christian and become vegetarian for religious reasons often suggest that the principles of love, mercy, and compassion should be extended to animals.

Ancient Hindus believed that humans should not kill in order to live—living a vegetarian lifestyle is a means of limiting cruelty or violence to other living things. One of the most important principles of Buddhism is to coexist peacefully with the world around us. Living a vegetarian lifestyle is the result of mercy and compassion for animals; it is also tied in to the idea of karma. Karma is the belief that your actions in this life will affect your station in the next life. A common saying in Buddhist culture is that "good is rewarded with good; evil is rewarded with evil."

Judaism also provides support for a plant-based diet. In the first chapter of Genesis, it is written that "God said, 'Behold, I have given you every plant yielding seed that is on the surface of all the earth, and every tree which has fruit yielding seed; it shall be food for you" (Gen. 1:29). Upon his creation, Adam was charged with the duty of naming and caring for the animals God created—it was not said that these animals were created as food for humans.

People switch to a vegetarian diet for a variety of different reasons. One single reason is not superior to another and, in many cases, all of the motivations listed previously contribute to an individual's decision to make the switch. Ultimately, the decision is yours to make: You need to decide where you stand on these issues and whether vegetarianism might be a fitting lifestyle for you. Before you make a decision, take the time to learn as much as you can about vegetarianism so you know exactly what you are getting into.

TWO

Meat the Press—Pitfalls of the Modern Western Diet

The vegetarian diet is completely meat-free. You probably already know what that means (abstaining from the consumption of beef, poultry, seafood, and other meat products), but do you know why it is important? Abstaining from meat is about more than refusing to support animal cruelty; it is also about achieving a healthy, natural diet. There are a number of significant health risks associated with meat consumption and other aspects of the modern Western diet. Before you can completely make the switch to a vegetarian lifestyle, you need to know *why* you are doing it and *how* it will benefit you.

Dangers of the Western Diet

American culture seems to be built on a foundation of fast food restaurants and processed-food companies. Millions of people subsist on a diet of frozen dinners, takeout food, and boxed meals, and this has had a significant impact on the health of our nation as a whole. The modern Western diet does not just affect Americans, however; fast food restaurants have spread throughout the globe, and in some countries eating fast food has become a status symbol—a means of participating in American culture.

You may not realize how dangerous the modern Western diet is because you have spent most of your life immersed in it. If you examine the facts, however, you will see that a diet founded on processed foods will never achieve the kind of health and wellness you desire. In this chapter you will not only learn the dangers of the modern Western diet, but you will also receive hard facts and evidence regarding the negative health effects of meat consumption. All of this should support your decision to make the switch to a vegetarian lifestyle.

THE MOST COMMON DANGERS ASSOCIATED WITH THE MODERN WESTERN DIET INCLUDE:

- It is very high in calorie-dense foods—foods that are high in calories but comparatively low in nutrients.
- It is centered on processed foods, which are high in sodium, saturated fat, and refined carbohydrates.
- It is often very low in nutrient-rich foods (i.e., fruits, vegetables, whole grains, etc.).
- High intake of refined carbohydrates can result in increased insulin production, which may lead to weight gain and obesity.
- It is very high in simple carbohydrates versus complex carbohydrates—our ancestors consumed 19 to 35 percent carbohydrates (primarily complex), while modern diets consist of 55 to 60 percent carbohydrates (primarily simple).
- Frequent consumption of processed foods and refined carbohydrates has been linked to increased rates of depression and anxiety.

- Foods often contain ingredients like peanuts, wheat, and soy, which can cause serious allergic reactions in sensitive or intolerant individuals.
- Processed foods disrupt healthy gut bacteria, providing an opening for disease and harmful bacteria.

Diseases Associated with Meat Consumption

A recent study, the results of which were featured in the March 12, 2012, *New York Times*, followed the eating habits of more than 120,000 individuals over the course of 25 years (Pan et al. 2012). During this 25-year period, almost 24,000 of the study participants passed away—about 5,900 from cardiovascular disease and almost 9,500 from cancer. The results of the study suggest that individuals who consumed red meat on a frequent basis had a 12 percent greater risk of dying than those who did not (Pan et al. 2012). This is largely due to the fact that those who frequently consume red meat are also more likely to smoke, to be less physically active, and to have a higher body mass index (BMI).

This study, published in the *Archives of Internal Medicine*, is just one of many that have provided support for the argument that meat consumption is unhealthy. There is a great deal of controversy regarding whether the benefits of meat consumption outweigh the risks. Many health professionals advocate for the consumption of red meat because it is a source of complete proteins, which are essential for healthy renewal and repair of the body. Red meat is also a good source of iron, zinc, and B vitamins. Proponents of plant-based diets, on the other hand, argue that red meat is often high in saturated fat, low in fiber, and often treated with growth hormones and other chemicals, which could be harmful to human health.

In order to truly understand the health benefits of a vegetarian lifestyle, you must first understand the problems associated with a meat-based diet. The overconsumption of meat in Western cultures has been linked to increased risk for cancer, heart disease, type 2 diabetes, and a number of other serious health conditions. Following you will find an in-depth explanation of some of the most common maladies associated with the consumption of meat.

DISEASES MOST COMMONLY ASSOCIATED WITH THE OVERCONSUMPTION OF MEAT:

- Cardiovascular disease
- Cancer
- Type 2 diabetes
- Bone disease
- Obesity
- Cognitive decline

CARDIOVASCULAR DISEASE

It has long been suggested that the saturated fat and cholesterol content of red meat contributes to increased risk for heart disease, but a recent article published in the journal *Nature Medicine* suggests that there may be an additional factor. L-carnitine is a compound found in abundance in red meat—the consumption of this compound results in the production of another compound in the gut called trimethylamine-N-oxide (TMAO). Studies conducted using mice have shown that TMAO causes atherosclerosis, which often results in clogged arteries and contributes to an increased risk for heart attack (Murphy et al. 2013).

CANCER

According to the World Health Organization, dietary factors are to blame for at least 30 percent of all cancers seen in modern Western culture. When researchers first began to study the correlation between diet and disease, studies conducted in Europe showed that individuals who followed a vegetarian diet were almost 40 percent less likely to develop cancer than were individuals who regularly consumed meat (Barnard et al. 1995). In the United States, a similar study was performed using a group of Seventh-Day Adventists.

Seventh-Day Adventists generally abstain from alcohol and tobacco products, and about half of the population follows a vegetarian diet. This allowed researchers to isolate the effects of meat consumption from other dietary and lifestyle factors. The results of this study, published in the *Journal of Clinical and Experimental Pharmacology and Physiology* in May 1982, also suggested that those who avoided meat had a reduced risk for cancer (Rouse et al. 1982). In 2007, the American Institute for Cancer Research and the World Cancer Research Fund published a report titled

"Food, Nutrition, Physical Activity and the Prevention of Cancer: A Global Perspective." This report provides a review of the dietary and lifestyle habits of a variety of cultures in correlation to each culture's cancer risk. Using the scientific and medical evidence that had been discovered to date, a panel of scientists judged certain factors on their potential to modify the risk of cancer. This panel found that the evidence suggesting red meats and processed meats are a cause of colorectal cancer is convincing. Evidence was also suggestive that red meats, processed meats, and animal foods containing iron contribute to increased risk for cancer of the lung, pancreas, stomach, prostate, esophagus, and endometrium (World Cancer Research Fund 2007).

TYPE 2 DIABETES

Type 2 diabetes occurs when the body's insulin secretion becomes impaired; as a result, the body is unable to control blood glucose levels, which can lead to dangerous spikes and crashes in blood sugar. Frank Hu, a professor of nutrition and epidemiology at the Harvard School of Public Health, states that there are three components in red meat which contribute to an increased risk for diabetes: sodium, nitrates, and iron. Sodium, found in table salt and processed meats, has been shown to increase blood pressure and may also cause insulin resistance. Insulin resistance occurs when the body fails to respond appropriately to the production of insulin. This often leads to the overproduction of insulin and a condition called hyperglycemia.

Like sodium, both nitrites and nitrates have been shown to induce a similar reaction; they may also impair the ability of pancreatic beta cells to function normally. The third component, iron, is a mineral that is essential for the healthy function of the human body. In high levels, however, it can lead to oxidative stress, cell damage, and chronic inflammation. This is especially dangerous for individuals with hereditary hemochromatosis—a condition in which the digestive tract absorbs too much iron. Heme iron, the type of easily absorbed iron found in red meat, is instrumental in causing beta cell damage.

BONE DISEASES

Studies have shown that overconsumption of red meat can have an adverse effect on the health of your bones for a number of reasons. One reason is that meat products, when compared to vegetable foods, tend to contain more phosphorus than calcium. Unbalanced phosphorus/calcium ratios can lead to hyperparathyroidism, a condition that leads to hypocalcaemia, which, if left untreated, often leads to bone disease. The process of digesting red meat can also have a damaging effect on your body. The process through which meat-based proteins are digested leaves acidic residue in the body. These acids need to be neutralized with alkalizing minerals and, if your diet doesn't contain enough of these minerals, they may be leeched from your bones.

OBESITY

According to a study conducted at the Johns Hopkins Bloomberg School of Public Health, overconsumption of meat may increase your risk for becoming obese (Wang and Beydoun 2009). This information conflicts with the principles of high-protein diets such as the Atkins diet. Studies have shown, however, that such high-protein diets do not provide long-term results. For instance, Atkins diet participants often experience reversed or stalled weight loss after as little as six months on the program. In contrast to meat-based diets, vegetarian diets are naturally low in fat, which helps reduce your caloric intake and manage your weight. Recent research suggests that meat-eaters have an obesity rate of three times that of vegetarians and nine times that of vegans; on average, an adult following the vegan diet weighs 10 to 20 pounds less than an adult following a meat-based diet.

COGNITIVE DECLINE

Throughout the course of your life, the mineral iron gradually accumulates in your cells and tissues. This buildup can eventually lead to free radical damage and mitochondrial decay. Dr. George Bartzokis, professor of psychology at UCLA, states that excess iron in the brain "contributes to the development of abnormal deposits of proteins associated with several prevalent neuro-degenerative diseases, such as Alzheimer's disease, Parkinson's disease and dementia" (Bartzokis et al. 2011). Even adults who do not suffer from any of these diseases may still exhibit decreased cognitive abilities in connection with higher brain iron levels.

In 2011, along with a number of his colleagues, Bartzokis published the results of a study regarding the connection between hysterectomy and increased iron levels in the brain. Though the results of the study are primarily focused on the link between premenopausal hysterectomy and the onset of neurodegenerative disease, they can also be used as support for the argument that the consumption of red meat is bad for your health.

According to the Academy of Nutrition and Dietetics, the recommended daily intake for iron is no more than 18 mg for females aged 19 to 50 years and 8 mg for males older than 19 years. A single 3-ounce serving of lean sirloin beef contains about 3 mg of iron. Many people, when they eat a steak, eat more than the recommended serving size—often two or three times more. Studies suggest that men tend to consume more red meat than women, and a single large steak could put you over your daily recommended dose of iron. The overconsumption of red meat throughout the course of an entire lifetime is likely to result in excess iron buildup in the brain, which increases your risk for developing neurodegenerative diseases like Alzheimer's disease and Parkinson's disease (Anderson 2012).

THREE

Veg Out—The Benefits of Going Vegetarian

For many people, making the switch to a vegetarian diet is done out of concern for animal rights. While this motivation is by no means a bad one, it is not the only thing to consider. The vegetarian lifestyle is incredibly beneficial in a number of ways—as much for you as it is for the animals whose lives you may be trying to save. Many cultures around the world subsist on primarily plant-based diets; that is, meat is not as readily available or as heavily consumed in other countries as it is in the United States. In cultures where people eat a largely plant-based diet, they tend to exhibit reduced risk for serious health conditions, including heart disease, diabetes, and cancer. In this chapter you will learn all of the benefits you can look forward to in switching to a vegetarian diet, including the health benefits that a vegetarian diet has over meat-based diets like the modern Western diet.

Overview of Vegetarian Health Benefits

The vegetarian lifestyle has been linked to a variety of significant health benefits from reduced risk for disease to improved nutrition. The following list provides a brief overview of the health benefits of going vegetarian.

HEALTH BENEFITS

- Reduced risk for several types of cancer, including lung cancer and colorectal cancer
- May help to prevent type 2 diabetes due to fiber and complex carbohydrate content
- Improved skin health and appearance due to antioxidant-rich plant foods
- Reduced exposure to artificial additives and chemicals
- Emphasis on fruits and vegetables, which are free from hormones that can be harmful for human consumption
- Could stop or reverse the effects of several significant health conditions, including cancer and heart disease
- Results in an increased consumption of fruits and vegetables, which may help to prevent macular degeneration and could slow cognitive decline

NUTRITIONAL BENEFITS

- High in potassium, which helps reduce acidity and support healthy kidney function
- Naturally low in sodium and saturated fat—may help lower cholesterol and reduce risk for heart disease
- High in vitamins and minerals in natural combinations for optimal absorption
- Reduced risk of food-borne illness
- High in magnesium, which helps the body properly absorb calcium for strong bones
- Increased intake of vitamin C, which is essential for immune system health

PHYSICAL BENEFITS

- Improved energy levels—body spends less energy digesting animal protein so energy can be used more efficiently
- Can greatly improve digestion, helping you feel more regular
- May help increase life span due to decreased exposure to harmful toxins and chemicals found in meat products
- More likely to promote and maintain a healthy weight and BMI
- May help ease the symptoms of menopause
- Increased bone health due to intake of magnesium and calcium
- Fairly easy to follow—much easier than the diet recommended by the American Diabetic Association for type 2 diabetes
- Could help improve bad breath and body odor by eliminating meat from the diet
- May help improve hair and nail growth as well as appearance

Pro-meat vs. Meat-free

The information provided in the previous chapter should give you an understanding of how and why the consumption of meat can be damaging to your health. In order to truly understand the vegetarian diet, however, you need to be able to correlate the negative effects of a meat-based diet with the benefits of a plant-based diet. In this section you will learn the extent to which meat consumption can increase your risk for serious disease while eating a diet based on plant foods can decrease your risk.

HEART DISEASE

The American Heart Association (AHA) identifies saturated fat and cholesterol as two of the primary factors contributing to increased risk for heart disease. Saturated fat is found in animal foods and dairy products; these foods also contain cholesterol. The AHA recommends a daily intake of saturated fat equal to less than 7 percent of your total daily calories, and cholesterol intake should be limited to 300 mg per day.

There are two types of dietary cholesterol—high-density lipoprotein (HDL) and low-density lipoprotein (LDL)—and it is important to maintain a healthy balance of both. HDL, or good cholesterol, should be higher than LDL, bad cholesterol. Every 1 percent reduction in cholesterol levels results in a 2 percent reduction in your risk for heart disease.

CANCER

There are a number of hypotheses regarding the connection between meat consumption and increased cancer risk. One hypothesis is that meat often contains certain carcinogenic compounds which may increase an individual's risk for developing cancer. Some of these compounds such as heterocyclic amines (HCA) and polycyclic aromatic hydrocarbons (PAH) are formed when meat is cooked or processed, and both of these compounds have been linked to increased cancer risk.

The high saturated fat content of meat may also increase your body's hormone production, which could also increase your risk for hormone-related cancers, namely breast cancer and prostate cancer. The Physicians Committee for Responsible Medicine published a report titled "Meat Consumption and Cancer Risk," which summarized the findings of numerous case-control and cohort studies regarding the connection between diet and cancer risk. In this report, it is noted that women who consume meat on a daily basis have a risk of breast cancer almost nine times higher than women who rarely eat meat. This report also references a study involving more than 148,000 adult participants whose dietary habits were followed since 1982—the individuals who had the highest intake of red and processed meats showed up to 50 percent higher risk for colon cancer than other groups.

A study conducted in the United Kingdom, and published in the journal *Cancer Epidemiology, Biomarkers & Prevention*, was performed to gauge the impact of a vegetarian diet on the risk for cancer. Compared with those who consumed meat on a regular basis, vegetarians showed a 10 percent reduced risk for cancer in general. The results of the study also showed a correlation between a vegetarian diet and reduced risk for stomach cancer, esophageal cancer, colon cancer, and pancreatic cancer. When the results between the different types of vegetarian diet were compared, those who followed a vegan diet were shown to have the most significant reduction in cancer risk (Tantamango-Bartley et al. 2013).

TYPE 2 DIABETES

A recent study published in the *Journal of the American Medical Association Internal Medicine* provides new evidence to support the hypothesis that consumption of red meat increases the risk for type 2 diabetes (Pan et al. 2013). This study was conducted by researchers at the National University of Singapore using data collected from almost 150,000 individuals. The results of the study suggest that increased consumption of red meat correlates to a 48 percent increase in risk for diabetes, while reduced consumption correlates to a 14 percent decrease in risk for diabetes (Pan et al. 2013). The study also found that substituting whole grains and nuts for meat helped to substantially lower the risk for diabetes.

COGNITIVE DECLINE

One of the most serious forms of cognitive decline is the neurodegenerative disease known as Alzheimer's. This disease is not a natural result of aging; it is caused by damage to and death of brain cells. Recent research suggests that there may be a correlation between the saturated fat and cholesterol found in animal products and the risk for neurodegenerative diseases like Alzheimer's and Parkinson's.

A study conducted by the Vanderbilt School of Medicine and published in the *American Journal of Medicine* in 2006 provides support for the hypothesis that vegetable-based diets help reduce cognitive decline. More than 1,800 participants in the study were followed for one year and evaluated based on their consumption of fruit and vegetable juices. Individuals who drank juices at least three times per week showed a hazard ratio for Alzheimer's disease of 0.24 while those who drank juice less than once a week had a ratio of 0.84 (Dai et al. 2006). The results of other studies indicate that the antioxidants found in a vegetarian diet can help reduce or reverse the damaging effects of free radicals in the brain, slowing or preventing numerous forms of cognitive decline.

BONE DISEASES

In 2001, the *American Journal of Clinical Nutrition* conducted a study regarding the correlation between an increased ratio of dietary animal to vegetable protein and increased risk for bone loss and fracture (Sellmeyer et al. 2001). This study followed a group of 1,035 postmenopausal women, measuring their protein intake via questionnaire and their bone mineral density by x-ray. The results of the study showed that women who consumed a high ratio of animal to vegetable protein experienced more rapid bone loss in the neck as well as a risk for hip fracture almost four times higher than those who consumed animal protein at a lower ratio to vegetable protein (Sellmeyer et al. 2001).

Another study, published in the *European Journal of Nutrition* in 2001, studied the correlation between diet and bone mineral density (Tucker et al. 2001). It was hypothesized that a fruit-and-vegetable-based diet would show correlation to higher bone mineral density at the start of the study and reduced bone loss over the course of the study. The results of the study did indeed support the hypothesis: Individuals who consumed more plant-based proteins exhibited greater bone mineral density and experienced lower bone loss over the four years covered in the study (Tucker et al. 2001).

OBESITY

The results of the study conducted at the Johns Hopkins Bloomberg School of Public Health regarding meat consumption and obesity yielded results to support the hypothesis that meat consumption is linked to BMI and central obesity. The data showed that individuals who consumed more meat on a regular basis were 33 percent more likely to have central obesity than those who ate less meat (Wang and Beydoun 2009). Additionally, higher intakes of meat products were associated with higher BMI and waist circumference measurements. In contrast, participants who exhibited higher fruit and vegetable intake had lower BMI and waist circumference measurements (Wang and Beydoun 2009).

Practical Reasons to Make the Switch

By now you have heard numerous reasons to switch to a vegetarian diet based on the ethical and medical merits of the decision. You may be surprised to find, however, that going vegetarian can be a practical choice as well. Some of the practical benefits of vegetarianism include:

- Switching to a vegetarian diet will make your palate much more sensitive to subtle flavors. In effect, you will get more enjoyment out of the food you eat once you cut out the meat.
- You can significantly reduce your grocery bill by removing meat and other animal products from your diet. Rather than spending 15 dollars on 1 pound of meat good for one meal, you can get several pounds of fresh produce that could last you several days.
- You will feel better. Although this has already been mentioned as a physical benefit of vegetarianism, it is also a practical reason to make the switch—who doesn't want to feel healthy?
- Vegetarianism is much more sustainable than factory farming. It takes about 7 pounds of grain to produce 1 pound of beef. Those 7 pounds of grain can go a lot further in feeding people than a single pound of beef.
- Your body doesn't need meat. Nutritionists have proven that you can get all the protein your body needs from vegetarian sources.

FOUR

Become an Herbivore— Making the Transition

Making the switch to a vegetarian diet may be the best choice you ever make. Because it is such a life-changing decision, it is important that you go about it correctly. Switching to a vegetarian diet should be done gradually so your body has time to adjust to the changes—the more gradual you make the transition, the easier you will find it to stick to the diet in the long term. In this chapter you will learn how to transform your kitchen into a vegetarian-friendly zone by removing nonvegetarian foods and stocking up on the staples of your new diet. You will also learn how to ease into the vegetarian lifestyle while assessing your progress along the way. Finally, you will receive 10 helpful tips to make your transition as smooth as possible.

Kitchen Clean-Out

Before you start your new vegetarian diet, you may need to clean out your pantry. You can choose to simply finish the animal food products you have in stock before restocking with vegetarian-friendly food items. If you want to get started right away, another option is to give away the animal food products you have to family, friends, or your local food pantry. Even though you have chosen to no longer consume these items, it is better to give the food away than to let it go to waste.

Once you are ready to get going with your vegetarian diet, use the checklist below to clean out your kitchen and pantry of nonvegetarian food items. You'll notice that some of the items on the list are quite obvious—a steak is certainly not part of a vegetarian diet. But you might be surprised to learn that some foods, particularly processed foods, contain hidden meat products. For example, some alcoholic products contain isinglass, a fish-based substance used in the clarification process. Gelatin, which is a protein gathered from cow and pig bones, can be found in a variety of foods from candy to marshmallows. To better understand how to read food labels to identify vegetarian-friendly foods, see "How to Read Food Labels" (page 48).

BEVERAGES

- ☐ Soda/pop products containing ester gum
- ☐ Beer and wine containing isinglass
- ☐ Orange juice with omega-3 fatty acids from fish products
- ☐ Red grapefruit juice containing carmine

FROZEN FOODS

- ☐ Prepared entrées

REFRIGERATED FOODS

- ☐ Deli meat
- ☐ Bacon
- ☐ Sausages
- ☐ Biscuits and rolls
- ☐ European cheeses
- ☐ Yogurt containing gelatin
- ☐ Margarine

MEAT AND SEAFOOD

- ☐ Beef
- ☐ Pork
- ☐ Poultry
- ☐ Wild game
- ☐ Canned fish
- ☐ Smoked fish
- ☐ Fresh fish
- ☐ Clams
- ☐ Mussels
- ☐ Shrimp
- ☐ Scallops

SNACK FOODS

- ☐ Jell-O snacks
- ☐ Red candies
- ☐ Gummy candies
- ☐ Potato chips with powdered cheese
- ☐ Hot Pockets
- ☐ French fries cooked in lard or shortening
- ☐ Cereal bars
- ☐ Marshmallows

CANNED/DRIED GOODS

- ☐ Many canned soups
- ☐ Refried beans with animal shortening
- ☐ Chicken broth
- ☐ Beef broth
- ☐ Condiments
- ☐ Caesar salad dressing
- ☐ Honey
- ☐ Oyster sauce
- ☐ Worcestershire sauce

- ☐ Fish sauce
- ☐ Some steak sauces
- ☐ Cake mix
- ☐ Chewing gum
- ☐ Seafood broth
- ☐ Refined white sugar
- ☐ Jams and jellies containing carmine
- ☐ Refined brown sugar

Vegetarian Grocery Shopping

After making the switch to a vegetarian lifestyle, your first trip to the grocery store may be a little overwhelming. This grocery shopping guide will help you find the necessities for a healthy vegetarian diet while also providing you with plenty of meal options. Don't be tempted to think that just because you are eliminating meat from your diet that you are limiting your choices. There are countless delicious fruit and vegetables out there just waiting for you to discover them. The grocery list on the following pages will help get you started on your new vegetarian lifestyle.

BREADS AND GRAINS

- ☐ Wild or brown rice
- ☐ Whole grains (millet, quinoa, etc.)
- ☐ Whole-grain breads
- ☐ Whole-grain pastas
- ☐ Brown-rice pastas
- ☐ Whole-wheat couscous

DESSERT OPTIONS

- ☐ Soy or rice nondairy desserts
- ☐ Fruit sorbets and sherbet
- ☐ Tofutti ice cream

CANNED GOODS

- ☐ Organic beans and vegetables
- ☐ Pasta sauces

BREAKFAST ITEMS

- ☐ Organic frozen waffles
- ☐ Organic steel-cut and instant oats

DAIRY/MILK REPLACEMENTS

- ☐ Rice, almond, soy, oat, or hemp milk
- ☐ Tofutti cream cheese/sour cream

REFRIGERATED FOOD ITEMS

- ☐ Tofurky deli slices/sausages
- ☐ Gardein products
- ☐ Lightlife Smart Dogs
- ☐ Vegetarian ice cream
- ☐ Chocolate (bittersweet or 72 percent dark)
- ☐ Vegetable broth
- ☐ Organic cereals
- ☐ Daiya cheese products
- ☐ Ener-G Egg Replacer
- ☐ Tempeh and tofu
- ☐ Fresh hummus
- ☐ Fresh salsa
- ☐ Frozen produce items
- ☐ Morning Star Farms products
- ☐ Nate's Meatless Meatballs
- ☐ Amy's frozen entrées

FRUITS AND VEGETABLES

- ☐ Seasonal produce
- ☐ Avocados
- ☐ Broccoli
- ☐ Fresh greens and lettuce
- ☐ Brussels sprouts
- ☐ All varieties of mushrooms

SNACK OPTIONS

- ☐ Fresh salsa or vegan dip
- ☐ Clif Bars
- ☐ Vegetable corn chips
- ☐ Popcorn
- ☐ Nut butters

EASING INTO THE TRANSITION

- ☐ Kashi vegan entrées
- ☐ BOCA burgers/Gardenburgers
- ☐ Meat-free crumbles
- ☐ All types of potatoes
- ☐ Apples
- ☐ Oranges and tangerines
- ☐ All types of melons
- ☐ All types of berries
- ☐ Dried fruit and fruit chips
- ☐ Trail mix
- ☐ Dried fruit
- ☐ Raw or toasted nuts
- ☐ Brown rice cakes

Switching to a vegetarian diet can be an exciting time, but it is not something you should do too quickly. If you make the switch too quickly, it could have negative effects on your body and it could make it more difficult for you to stick to the vegetarian diet in the long run. Even though most people do not eat exactly the same meals every day, we all have our habits. If you suddenly make a drastic change to your diet, it could put stress on your digestive system, especially if you suddenly increase your intake of dietary fiber.

The key to going vegetarian gradually is to make small changes to your diet over a significant period of time. Your first step, rather than cutting out all animal products right from the start, should be to add more fruits, vegetables, grains, and legumes to your diet. You might also think about reducing the amount of meat you use in your recipes to balance out the extra vegetables. Next, try eliminating meat from one meal a day or several meals a week. After a few weeks of this, try incorporating some meatless substitutes in your favorite recipes—try vegan crumbles in place of meat in your spaghetti sauce, or tofu in your stir-fry.

If you have chosen to be a vegan, you will also need to remove eggs, cheese, and other dairy products from your diet. For many people, cheese is the hardest thing to give up, so you may want to save that for last. Start out by replacing dairy milk with dairy-free alternatives such as soy milk, almond milk, and coconut milk. Start using egg replacer in your baking recipes and try to reduce the amount of cheese you use on a regular basis. When you are ready, swap out cheese for vegan-friendly alternatives like Daiya products and soy cheese. If you make the transition into a vegan lifestyle slow and methodical, your body will have time to adjust to the changes and you won't feel like you are suddenly depriving yourself of all the foods you have gotten used to consuming.

Self-Assessment During Your Transition

For many people, making the transition into a vegetarian lifestyle is a rewarding process, so you may want to keep a journal to track your progress. Some of the most common reasons for switching to a vegetarian diet include losing weight or improving health. If this is the case with you, record your body weight and measurements before you start the transition into a vegetarian lifestyle and retake your measurements every two weeks or so. You may also want to take note of other physical changes you experience, such as clearer skin, shinier hair, and stronger nails.

Many people who make the switch to a vegetarian diet notice dramatic improvements in their energy levels and overall well-being. Take note of your energy level throughout the day—does it fluctuate throughout the day or has it started to level out, leaving you feeling refreshed and energized all day long? You may also experience some psychological changes—you may find yourself feeling more positive. You will no longer feel as if your mind is controlled by thoughts of food or that you are simply eating for the sake of eating, not actually enjoying the food you eat.

A surprising change you may also notice is that food begins to become more flavorful. You might think that making so many eliminations from your diet would have the opposite effect, but for many people, going vegetarian results in food becoming more enjoyable and more flavorful. Every person's experience will be different in transitioning into a vegetarian lifestyle. To truly realize the benefits and changes you experience personally, you should take the time to keep a journal or a log of your daily progress. Not only will this help you to see how far you have come, but it will also be a great tool to use in sharing your vegetarian lifestyle with others.

MAKING THE RIGHT CHOICES

Your success in switching to a vegetarian diet depends on your making the right choices when it comes to food. One of the most common mistakes new vegetarians make is relying on prepared foods and snacks. Even though these foods may be vegetarian-friendly, they may also be full of empty calories that do not actually provide your body with much nutrition. Living a healthy and balanced vegetarian lifestyle will require you to do some cooking for yourself at home so you get the full nutritional benefit of the foods you are eating.

Another mistake people make in switching to a vegetarian diet is not eating enough. It is important to remember that fruits and vegetables contain fewer calories (but more nutrients) than animal products, so you may need to eat higher quantities of food to feel full. On a related note, you should always carry with you some vegetarian-friendly snacks like dried fruit or nuts so you have something to munch on when you get hungry. If you have healthy snacks on hand, you will be less likely to go for unhealthy options when you are desperate for something to eat.

PRACTICAL TIPS FOR A SUCCESSFUL TRANSITION

- Take the opportunity to try new things. Many cultures follow vegetarian or near-vegetarian diets, so go out and try some ethnic food. Try some

Indian vegetable curries, Mediterranean hummus and falafel, and Japanese sushi.

- Check the freezer section at your grocery store for meatless burgers, "hot dogs," "chicken patties," and more. These products are a great option for a quick meal, and they can be very helpful in making the transition to a meat-free lifestyle.
- Start off slow. Don't try to rush the transition to a vegetarian lifestyle, because sudden increased consumption of dietary fiber could put stress on your digestive system. Instead, try adding some extra vegetables to your favorite meals to replace some or all of the meat.
- Stock up on vegetarian cookbooks. The beauty of living a vegetarian lifestyle is that the options are endless when it comes to unique and flavorful combinations of ingredients. Check out a few cookbooks from the library to get yourself started or visit the PETA website for free recipes.
- Take out your apron and unpack your pots and pans. For people who are not used to cooking much for themselves, it can be tempting to live almost entirely off of frozen vegetarian entrées. While these options are great for a quick meal, it is essential that you learn how to cook some basic meals for yourself because whole foods are the most nutritious when they are fresh.
- Do some research. Whatever your motives are for switching to a vegetarian lifestyle, read up on the issues that most interest you. Your friends and family are likely to have questions, so you should be prepared to answer them. Learning everything you can about animal rights and the health benefits of a vegetarian lifestyle will also help to keep you motivated.
- Try planning your meals as you get used to the vegetarian diet. It can be difficult at first to achieve the proper balance of macronutrients, vitamins, and minerals in a plant-based diet. Planning your meals

ahead of time will help you to get all of the nutrients your body needs on a daily basis.

- Familiarize yourself with Internet databases such as VegGuide.org and HappyCow.net to find vegetarian- and vegan-friendly restaurants in your area. You might want to make up a short list and keep it in your purse or car so you have it when you need to pick up or stop for a quick meal.

- Team up with a friend, join an online program, or find a vegetarian activist group in your community for support and help with the transition. If you have a spouse or partner who is willing to make the switch with you, the two of you will be able to help each other through the transition.

- Browse some vegan and vegetarian forums online. There are a number of forums and community chat boards available online that provide vegetarians with a means of sharing recipes, asking/answering questions, and simply providing support for one another. Some popular forums include VeganForum.com, HappyCow.net, and VegTalk.org.

FIVE

Challenges and Caveats

Switching to a new diet is always a challenge, especially if it requires you to change nearly all of your eating habits. While the vegetarian diet may seem incredibly restrictive if you are used to picking up takeout or going through the drive-through for most of your meals, it is really not that difficult to follow. In this chapter you will learn how to deal with some of the challenges of switching to a vegetarian diet. You will learn about some of the nutritional deficiencies you need to be careful to avoid, and you will receive tips on how to read food labels; how to enjoy meals with friends and family; and how to find vegetarian-friendly options when eating out.

Avoiding Nutritional Deficiencies

The key to a healthy vegetarian diet is achieving a balance of nutrients—eating a wide assortment of fruits, vegetables, leafy greens, nuts, whole grains, and legumes will help to provide your body with all of the nutrients it needs.

The following chart identifies the daily requirements for some of the nutrients vegetarian diets are often found to be lacking:

Daily Nutritional Requirements

NUTRIENT	CHILDREN	AVERAGE MALE	AVERAGE FEMALE
PROTEIN	11 grams	56 grams	46 grams
FAT	30 grams	15 to 20 percent of daily calories	15 to 20 percent of daily calories
CALCIUM	800 milligrams	800 milligrams	800 milligrams
VITAMIN D	10 micrograms	10 micrograms	10 micrograms
VITAMIN B_{12}	1.0 micrograms	2.0 micrograms	2.0 micrograms
IRON	4.1 milligrams	6.0 milligrams	8.1 milligrams
ZINC	4.0 milligrams	9.4 milligrams	6.8 milligrams

PROTEIN

Many people mistakenly assume that eliminating meat from your diet means that it will be difficult to achieve your daily recommended intake for protein. In fact, a well-balanced vegetarian diet is full of plant-based protein. You do not need to eat foods in certain combinations or plan your meals down to the very last detail to get your daily protein in—all you have to do is eat a varied diet. Most foods contain some level of protein, but the best sources for vegetarian protein include tofu, lentils, chickpeas, peanut butter, peas, soy milk, almonds, rice, spinach, potatoes, kale, and broccoli.

FAT

While saturated fats are unhealthy in large quantities, your body does require some monounsaturated fat in order to be healthy. Some good sources of healthy fats include avocado, nuts, nut butters, olive oil, seeds, and coconut. Fat should only account for 15 to 20 percent of your daily caloric intake, so use these foods sparingly.

CALCIUM

You probably grew up hearing that drinking milk is the key to building strong bones. In reality, milk may not be as high in calcium as you were led to believe. Calcium is, however, still an essential nutrient for maintaining bone health. This nutrient can be gleaned from a number of vegetarian sources, including dark green vegetables, fortified soy milk, fortified orange juice, tofu fortified with calcium sulfate, soybeans, tempeh, almond butter, broccoli, and bok choy. You may also want to consider taking a daily calcium supplement to make sure your daily need for calcium is met.

VITAMIN D

Vitamin D is actually a hormone, not a vitamin, and it plays a role in protecting bone health. The vegetarian diet does not naturally contain vitamin D so you will need to incorporate this nutrient into your diet. Some ways to get vitamin D include sun exposure, consumption of sun-exposed mushrooms, and dietary supplements. Many dietary supplements are not vegan-friendly, so look for a supplement that has ergocalciferol as the main ingredient.

VITAMIN B$_{12}$

This vitamin is typically derived from animal sources, and it is essential for maintaining healthy nerves and blood cells. Vitamin B$_{12}$ is not actually produced by animals but by bacteria in the plants and soil to which they are exposed. Some vegan sources of vitamin B$_{12}$ include fortified nutritional yeast, tempeh, miso, and sea vegetables. The amount of the vitamin in these foods varies depending on the method of processing, so it is always a good idea to take a nutritional supplement or multivitamin.

IRON

Iron is the nutrient responsible for helping to build strong muscles. This mineral is best absorbed by the body when eaten in combination with vitamin C. Some good sources of vegetarian iron include leafy green vegetables, soybeans, lentils, dried beans, tahini, peas, watermelon, and kale. Not only are leafy greens like kale, Swiss chard, and spinach good sources of iron, they also contain vitamin C, which helps your body absorb the iron more efficiently.

ZINC

This mineral plays an important role in maintaining immune system health and promoting healing of wounds. Zinc also supports healthy development in infants and children. Zinc can be found in a number of vegetarian sources, including whole grains, nuts, legumes, and fortified cereals.

How to Read Food Labels

Understanding the basics of food labeling will help you to easily identify foods that are vegetarian-friendly. Luckily, in 2006, the Food Standards Agency (FSA) made some changes to food labeling, making it easier to identify foods that are vegan or vegetarian. With help from the Vegetarian and Vegan Societies, official criteria for these terms were established. The official criteria for vegan and vegetarian foods as established by the FSA are as follows:

Vegan the term vegan should not be applied to foods that are, or are made from or with the aid of, animals or animal products (including products from living animals).

Vegetarian the term vegetarian should not be applied to foods that are, or are made from or with the aid of products, derived from animals that have died, have been slaughtered, or animals that die as a result of being eaten.

Animals include farmed, wild, or domestic animals, including livestock poultry, game, fish, shellfish, crustaceans, amphibians, tunicates, echinoderms, mollusks, and insects.

Even though criteria for the terms vegan and vegetarian have been established by the FSA, use of these terms is still voluntary. While many food companies have begun to identify their products as vegan or vegetarian, others do not and you must read the ingredients on the label to be sure. You also need to be aware that products can be mislabeled; if the company does not have a complete understanding of what it means to be vegetarian, they may label something as "suitable for vegetarians" when it really is not. Your first step in determining whether a product is vegetarian or not is to look for the Vegetarian Society trademark. Even if the product doesn't carry the trademark, it might still be vegetarian—you just have to read the ingredients to find out.

Interesting Fact: In the United Kingdom in 2010, the FSA guidelines establishing the criteria for vegan and vegetarian food were adopted in principle by the European Parliament. This means that UK residents can now bring a civil suit against manufacturers found to be misusing the term vegan or vegetarian.

FOOD PRODUCTS CONTAINING THE FOLLOWING INGREDIENTS ARE NOT VEGETARIAN:

- Allantoin
- Arachidonic acid
- Bone char or meal
- Carminic acid
- Caprylic acid
- Chitosan
- Cholesterol
- Collagen
- Disodium inosinate
- Elastin
- Fish oil
- Gelatin
- Guanine
- Hydrolyzed animal protein
- Insulin
- Isinglass
- Keratin
- Lanolin
- Lipase
- Monoglyceride
- Pepsin
- Pristane
- Progesterone
- Rennet
- Retinol
- Tallow

THE FOLLOWING INGREDIENTS MAY BE DERIVED FROM ANIMAL SOURCES, DEPENDING ON THE MANUFACTURER:

- Carbon black
- Colors and dyes
- Cysteine
- Glycerol
- Lactic acid
- Lecithins
- Myristic acid
- Oleic acid
- Potassium nitrate
- Stearic acid
- Sterols
- Urea

SHARING A MEAL WITH FAMILY AND FRIENDS

When a friend or family member invites you over for a meal, the last thing you want to do is offend them by not eating the food they have prepared. It is always a good idea to let your host know ahead of time that you are a vegetarian. If your host is willing to accommodate you, explain the requirements of the diet. You can also offer to bring a vegetarian dish to share—this option saves your host from having to change the menu and also gives you an opportunity to share vegetarian food with others. It may also be a good opportunity to share the reasons you switched to a vegetarian diet, potentially influencing others to make the same choice.

RESTAURANT CHAINS THAT HAVE MULTIPLE VEGETARIAN-FRIENDLY MENU OPTIONS:

- California Pizza Kitchen
- The Cheesecake Factory
- Chili's
- Chipotle Mexican Grill
- Hard Rock Café
- Johnny Rockets
- Kona Grill
- Mimi's Café
- Moe's Southwest Grill
- O'Naturals
- Panera Bread
- P.F. Chang's China Bistro
- Red Robin
- Romano's Macaroni Grill
- Roy Rogers
- Ruby Tuesday
- Starbucks
- Swenson's
- Sweet Tomatoes
- World Wrapps

FAST FOOD CHAINS THAT OFFER VEGETARIAN-FRIENDLY OPTIONS IN THE FORM OF SALADS AND/OR VEGGIE BURGERS:

- Arby's
- Burger King
- Quiznos
- Subway
- Taco Bell
- Wendy's

If you find yourself out with friends and family, there are several vegetarian-friendly options you can almost always count on. At Chinese restaurants, stick to vegetable or tofu dishes; you can also go with vegetable fried rice or vegetable lo mein. Many Mexican dishes can be made vegetarian-friendly by simply omitting the meat; try a bean burrito or make a meal out of refried beans and rice rolled up in fresh tortillas. When in doubt, you can always ask for a salad of chopped vegetables with a drizzle of olive oil and vinegar or a spritz of fresh lemon juice.

SIX

The Vegetarian Kitchen— Useful Tools and Appliances

Switching to a vegetarian diet will not only open up to you a world of new foods and flavors, but it will also introduce you to new cooking methods. You may not realize the variety of kitchen appliances available to you. In this chapter, you will learn about some useful kitchen appliances to have around to make the most of your new vegetarian diet.

Useful Kitchen Appliances

FOOD PROCESSOR

A food processor is a kitchen appliance that can be used to peel, chop, or purée foods. Food processors are similar in function to blenders, but they feature interchangeable blades and disks. A food processor is a valuable tool in the vegetarian kitchen because it can be used to chop vegetables for salads and salsas, to grind nuts, to shred vegetables, and to knead dough.

Benefits of Food Processors These appliances come in a variety of sizes ranging from mini 1½-cup processors to commercial grade 14-cup processors. Another benefit of food processors over blenders is that they do not require the addition of liquid as blenders do.

SLOW COOKER

A slow cooker is an electrical appliance that utilizes low temperatures to cook foods over an extended period of time. These appliances are typically ovular or circular in shape, and they come with a heavy glass or ceramic lid to lock in moisture during the cooking process. Some slow cookers even come with a removable insert that allows for easy transport of cooked food and cleaning of the appliance.

Benefits of Slow Cookers Slow cooking is the ideal cooking method for soups and stews because it preserves the moisture of the food while intensifying the flavor. One of the main benefits of slow cooking is that it is incredibly easy; in most cases all you need to do is combine the ingredients in the cooker and let it cook for several hours. If you lead a busy lifestyle, having a slow cooker will enable you to prepare a meal before leaving for work in the morning so that it is hot, ready, and waiting for you when you get home in the evening.

JUICER

A juicer is an appliance used to separate the juice in fruits and vegetables from the pulp; this process is called juicing. Juicing has become extremely popular in the modern health and fitness world as a means of detoxification and weight loss. It is also an excellent addition to a healthy vegetarian diet.

There are three different types of juicers: centrifugal juicers, masticating juicers, and triturating juicers. A centrifugal juicer is both easy to operate and easy to clean, making it one of the most popular types of juicer available. These juicers work by grinding the produce through a grated basket, separating the pulp from the juice. Masticating juicers are motor driven, and they work by kneading and grinding the raw material to extract the juice. These juicers work a little more slowly than other models, but they also operate at a lower heat to preserve the enzymes in the raw material. A triturating juicer utilizes a two-step process: the raw material is first crushed, then it is pressed to extract the juice.

Benefits of Juicing One of the main benefits of juicing is that it makes the nutrients in fresh fruits and vegetables easier for your body to absorb. It is also much easier to drink an 8-ounce glass of juice containing three or more servings of vegetables than it is to eat a large plate piled with veggies. Having a juicer in your kitchen will allow you to expand your recipe repertoire, enabling you to try new foods and to experiment with different flavors.

BLENDER

A blender, commonly referred to as a liquidizer in the United Kingdom, is an electrical appliance used to purée or emulsify foods. Having a high-quality blender in your kitchen will enable you to make your own fruit and vegetable smoothies at home.

Benefits of Smoothies The main benefit of smoothies over juices is that they retain their original dietary fiber content. The process of juicing removes the pulp and thus the fiber content from the raw materials. Blending the materials, on the other hand, preserves the fiber content. Healthy smoothies can be made using a variety of fruits and vegetables in whatever flavor combinations you like.

FOOD DEHYDRATOR

A food dehydrator is an appliance that uses heat and airflow to remove moisture from food. Most fruits and vegetables contain 80 to 95 percent water content. When that moisture is removed, it helps to prevent the growth of bacteria and also helps to prevent the food from spoiling. A food dehydrator can be used to make your own dried fruit slices at home to use in homemade trail mixes and other snacks or desserts.

Benefits of Dehydrators Food dehydrators come in a variety of styles. Most styles utilize stackable trays and incorporate either a solar or electric power source to provide heat. Dehydrating food, rather than cooking it with high heat, preserves the natural enzymes in the food.

MAGIC BULLET

The Magic Bullet is a small, compact blender produced by Homeland Housewares. This appliance typically comes with multiple blade attachments and mixing cups, which can be used for both blending and storing foods. A Magic Bullet can be used to chop or blend foods—it is great for making homemade sauces, dips, and smoothies.

Benefits of Magic Bullets One of the main benefits of Magic Bullets over traditional blenders is their compact size. These mini appliances do not take up much space in your kitchen and you are able to blend the ingredients in the same cup you will use to serve or store them. There are a number of optional cups and addons that can be used to chop or whip foods in addition to blending them.

SEED GRINDER

A seed grinder can be used to grind your own fresh seeds, nuts, and spices at home. Some of the most common uses for these appliances is grinding flaxseed, fresh peppercorns, and nuts for use in vegetarian recipes. Seed grinders come in a variety of shapes and sizes, from small electric grinders to large hand-operated grinders.

Benefits of Seed Grinding Having a seed grinder means that can grind small amounts of seeds, nuts, or spices as you need them. Ground flaxseed and other commonly used vegetarian foods tend to spoil quickly so, unless you use large quantities of these items, it may be more cost-effective to buy whole seed and grind the amount you need yourself. Seed grinders are also great for grinding your own spices, including peppercorns, nutmeg, and more—freshly ground spices have much more flavor than the bottled spices you find in the grocery store.

Part Two

THE RECIPES

Versatile Vegetarian Dishes and Meal Plans

SEVEN

Two-Week Vegetarian Meal Plan

In this chapter you will find 14 days' worth of meal plans. These meal plans are constructed using the recipes you will find in the following chapters. Feel free to mix and match the recipes to suit your preferences, and supplement your meals with the quick and easy snacks as suggested.

Day 1

Breakfast: Tomato Basil Omelet
Lunch: Lentil Soup
Dinner: Garlic Green Pepper Pasta
Dessert/Snacks: Raw Mixed Berry Pie,
Hummus with veggie sticks

Day 2

Breakfast: Chocolate Chip Pancakes
Lunch: Chopped Salad with Avocado
Dinner: Raw Mushroom Burger
Dessert/Snacks: Strawberry Apple Kale Smoothie,
Sliced apple with peanut butter

Day 3

Breakfast: Maple Raspberry Muffins
Lunch: Gazpacho
Dinner: Easy Fruit Sushi
Dessert/Snacks: Mango Peach Smoothie,
All-Natural Cheese

Day 4

Breakfast: Kiwi Strawberry Spinach Smoothie
Lunch: Strawberry Pecan Spring Salad
Dinner: Broccoli Casserole
Dessert/Snacks: Raw Chocolate Truffles,
Brown rice cake with almond butter

Day 5

Breakfast: Raisin Apple Breakfast Oats
Lunch: Chilled Avocado Soup
Dinner: Sesame Mango Avocado Salad
Dessert/Snacks: Berry Blast Juice,
Dry roasted peanuts

Day 6

Breakfast: Whole-Wheat Buttermilk Waffles
Lunch: Kale and Mushroom Soup
Dinner: Baked Eggplant Parmesan
Dessert/Snacks: Fruit Smoothie Pops,
Mixed fruit cup

Day 7

Breakfast: Refreshing Red Radish Juice
Lunch: Quinoa Salad with Lentils and Tomatoes
Dinner: Raw Stuffed Mushrooms
Dessert/Snacks: Berries and Cream Crêpes,
Baked vegetable chips

Day 8

Breakfast: Almond Butter Pancakes
Lunch: Sun-dried Tomato Spinach Salad
Dinner: Raw Cilantro Avocado Veggie Wraps
Dessert/Snacks: Raw Power Squares,
Yellow corn chips with salsa

Day 9

Breakfast: Spinach and Blue Cheese Omelet
Lunch: Creamy Cauliflower Soup
Dinner: Garlic Green Pepper Pasta
Dessert/Snacks: Raw Chocolate Milk,
Handful of whole-wheat crackers

Day 10

Breakfast: Strawberry Banana Overnight Oats
Lunch: Chopped Tomato and Avocado Salad
Dinner: Veggie Fried Rice
Dessert/Snacks: Blueberry Lime Sorbet,
Fresh orange slices

Day 11

Breakfast: Banana Walnut Muffins
Lunch: Tomato Basil Bisque
Dinner: Raw Stuffed Apples
Dessert/Snacks: Raw Banana Mint Pie,
Air-popped popcorn

Day 12

Breakfast: Steel-Cut Oatmeal with Dried Cranberries
Lunch: Broccoli Salad with Almonds
Dinner: Tropical Melon Fruit Cup
Dessert/Snacks: Raw Chocolate Chip Cookies,
Apple cinnamon rice cakes

Day 13

Breakfast: Pomegranate Pear Smoothie
Lunch: Curried Butternut Squash Stew
Dinner: Summer Squash Casserole
Dessert/Snacks: Blueberry Banana Coconut Smoothie,
Pita chips with hummus

Day 14

Breakfast: Power-Packed Green Juice
Lunch: Mandarin Spinach Salad with Walnuts
Dinner: Baked Eggplant Parmesan
Dessert/Snacks: Toast with Blueberry Jam,
Crackers with cheese slices

EIGHT

Breakfast

There are plenty of delicious options to choose from. Fresh smoothies and homemade juices, for example, are an excellent way to start your day. Packed with nutrients and refreshing flavor, these recipes are sure to wake you up. If you like to have something a little more substantial for breakfast, try a Tomato Basil Omelet, some Whole-Wheat Buttermilk Waffles, or a bowl of Cinnamon Oatmeal with Honey.

RECIPES

Morning Melon Agua Fresca

Serves 2 to 3

Agua fresca is Spanish for "fresh water," and it is traditionally made by combining fruit with flowers or seeds and water. This melon agua fresca is just what you need to wake up in the morning.

1 small honeydew or cantaloupe

½ lime, peeled

1½ cups water

1. Peel the melon and chop it to fit in the juicer.

2. Place a pitcher or plastic container under the spout of your juicer.

3. Feed the melon and lime through the juicer.

4. Stir the water into the juice and divide among glasses to serve.

Per Serving Calories 67; Total fat: 0g; Saturated fat: 0g; Total carbs: 18g; Fiber: 2g; Cholesterol: 0mg; Protein: 2g

Ginger Strawberry Beet Juice

Serves 2

Beets are an excellent source of choline, iron, potassium, and vitamin A. Fresh ginger is known for its detoxification qualities and for helping to support healthy digestion. All in all, this juice is packed with healthy nutrients!

1 cup fresh strawberries, halved

1 cup water

1 medium-sized beet, chopped

1 medium apple, cored and chopped

2 tablespoons fresh grated ginger

1. Combine the strawberries and water in a blender and blend until smooth.

2. Add the remaining ingredients and blend until well combined. Add more water, if needed, to thin.

3. Pour the juice into two glasses and serve.

Per Serving Calories 72; Total fat: 0g; Saturated fat: 0g; Total carbs: 21g; Fiber: 1g; Cholesterol: 0mg; Protein: 2g

Refreshing Red Radish Juice

Serves 2

Radishes aren't exactly a popular food, but they are incredibly good for you. Full of protein, vitamin C, and folic acid, radishes help fight cancer, soothe skin irritation, and treat kidney problems.

6 small radishes, greens included

1 cup baby spinach leaves

1 cup fresh strawberries

1 medium apple, halved

1 (½-inch) piece fresh ginger

1. Rinse all of the ingredients well and shake off the excess water.

2. Place a pitcher or plastic container under the spout of your juicer.

3. Feed the ingredients through a juicer, one at a time, in the order listed.

4. Stir the juice well.

5. Pour into two glasses and serve immediately.

Per Serving Calories 48; Total fat: 0g; Saturated fat: 0g; Total carbs: 14g; Fiber: 0g; Cholesterol: 0mg; Protein: 1g

Power-Packed Green Juice

This green juice is filled to the brim with protein. Not only is it full of healthy nutrients, but it also has great flavor!

1 bunch fresh curly kale

½ bunch collard greens

1 small head broccoli

1 large carrot

1 tablespoon ground flaxseed

1. Rinse the vegetables well and shake off the excess water.

2. Place a pitcher or plastic container under the spout of your juicer.

3. Feed the ingredients through a juicer, one at a time, in the order listed.

4. Stir the ground flaxseed into the juice well.

5. Pour into two glasses and serve immediately.

Per Serving Calories 119; Total fat: 3g; Saturated fat: 0g; Total carbs: 29g; Fiber: 2g; Cholesterol: 0mg; Protein: 13g

Bold Broccoli Basil Juice

Broccoli is a great source of dietary fiber and vitamin C. Combined with the fresh flavor of basil leaves, this juice will wake you up and keep you powered up all morning long.

1 cup fresh basil leaves

1 cup organic orange juice

2 cups broccoli florets

5 to 6 ice cubes

1. Place the basil leaves and orange juice in a blender.

2. Blend the mixture until smooth; then add the remaining ingredients.

3. Pulse to chop the broccoli and ice; blend until smooth.

4. Pour into two glasses and serve immediately.

Per Serving Calories 77; Total fat: 1g; Saturated fat: 0g; Total carbs: 21g; Fiber: 1g; Cholesterol: 0mg; Protein: 7g

Blackberry Green Tea Smoothie

Serves 2

If you prefer not to drink coffee but still need a little something to wake you up, this blackberry green tea smoothie is just what you need. With delicious blackberry flavor and a hint of caffeine, this smoothie will perk you up in no time.

1 cup green tea, brewed and cooled

½ cup fresh mint leaves

2 cups frozen blackberries

3 to 4 ice cubes, if desired

1. Place the green tea and mint leaves in a blender and blend until liquefied.

2. Add the remaining ingredients and pulse to chop the berries and ice cubes.

3. Blend the mixture until smooth.

4. Pour into two glasses and serve immediately.

Per Serving Calories 72; Total fat: 1g; Saturated fat: 0g; Total carbs: 16g; Fiber: 9g; Cholesterol: 0mg; Protein: 3g

Pomegranate Pear Smoothie

Serves 2

Pears are an excellent source of dietary fiber, and they also contain vitamin C and potassium. In this smoothie, pears provide a delicious balance to the pomegranate juice while also providing digestion-boosting benefits.

1 cup pomegranate juice

1 cup chopped kale leaves

2 fresh pears, peeled and chopped

5 to 6 ice cubes

1. Combine the pomegranate juice and kale in a blender and blend until smooth.

2. Add the remaining ingredients and blend until well combined. Add more ice cubes, if needed, to thicken.

3. Pour the smoothie into two glasses and serve immediately.

Per Serving Calories 188; Total fat: 0g; Saturated fat: 0g; Total carbs: 47g; Fiber: 6g; Cholesterol: 0mg; Protein: 2g

Kiwi Strawberry Spinach Smoothie

Serves 2

Kiwi contains high levels of vitamin C, which is essential for healing wounds and promoting dental health. This smoothie provides all of the health benefits of kiwi along with its delicious flavor.

1 cup fresh baby spinach

1 cup organic orange juice

1½ cups frozen strawberries

2 fresh kiwis, peeled and halved

4 to 5 ice cubes, if desired

1. Combine the spinach and orange juice in a blender and blend until liquefied.

2. Add the remaining ingredients and pulse to chop the frozen berries and ice cubes.

3. Blend the mixture until smooth.

4. Pour into two glasses and serve immediately.

Per Serving Calories 132; Total fat: 1g; Saturated fat: 0g; Total carbs: 31g; Fiber: 4g; Cholesterol: 0mg; Protein: 3g

Maple Raspberry Muffins

Makes 24 mini muffins • Serving size = 2 mini muffins

If you don't have much time to make breakfast in the morning, these maple raspberry muffins are a great option. Prepare them the night before and then freeze them. Thaw a few overnight to enjoy in the morning.

1 cup whole-wheat flour

¾ cup all-purpose flour

¼ cup wheat germ

1½ teaspoons baking soda

Pinch of salt

1 cup unsweetened coconut milk

1 tablespoon apple cider vinegar

½ cup pure maple syrup

¼ cup coconut oil, melted

1 teaspoon vanilla extract

1¼ cups fresh raspberries

1. Preheat oven to 375°F and line a 24-cup mini muffin pan with paper liners.

2. Whisk together the flours, wheat germ, baking soda, and salt in a mixing bowl. Set aside.

3. In a small bowl, combine the coconut milk and apple cider vinegar.

4. In a separate bowl, whisk together the maple syrup, coconut oil, and vanilla extract.

5. Gently beat the maple syrup mixture into the dry ingredients and stir until smooth and combined.

6. Whisk in the coconut milk mixture and then fold in the raspberries.

7. Immediately spoon the batter into the prepared muffin pan and bake for 15 to 20 minutes until a knife inserted in the center comes out clean.

8. Cool the muffins for about 10 minutes before serving.

Per Serving Calories 203; Total fat: 10g; Saturated fat: 8g; Total carbs: 27g; Fiber: 2g; Cholesterol: 0mg; Protein: 3g

Banana Walnut Muffins

Makes about 24 mini muffins • Serving size = 2 mini muffins

Banana walnut muffins are a classic flavor, but this recipe gives them a little twist by using whole-wheat flour. If a mini muffin isn't enough for you, feel free to use a standard muffin pan and add a few minutes to the baking time.

1¾ cups whole-wheat flour

¼ cup ground flaxseed

1½ teaspoons baking soda

1 teaspoon ground cinnamon

¼ teaspoon ground nutmeg

Pinch of salt

½ cup unsweetened coconut milk

1 tablespoon apple cider vinegar

1 ripe banana, mashed

½ cup pure maple syrup

¼ cup coconut oil, melted

1 teaspoon almond extract

¾ cup finely chopped walnuts

1. Preheat oven to 375°F and line a 24-cup mini muffin pan with paper liners.

2. Whisk together the flour, ground flaxseed, baking soda, cinnamon, nutmeg, and salt in a mixing bowl; set aside.

3. In a small bowl, combine the coconut milk and apple cider vinegar.

4. In a separate bowl, whisk together the banana, maple syrup, coconut oil, and almond extract.

5. Gently beat the maple syrup mixture into the dry ingredients and stir until smooth and combined.

6. Whisk in the coconut milk mixture until well combined and then fold in the walnuts.

7. Immediately spoon the batter into the prepared muffin pan and bake for 15 to 20 minutes until a knife inserted in the center comes out clean.

8. Cool the muffins for about 10 minutes before serving.

Per Serving Calories 235; Total fat: 12g; Saturated fat: 7g; Total carbs: 27g; Fiber: 2g; Cholesterol: 0mg; Protein: 4g

Cinnamon Oatmeal with Honey

Makes about 3 cups • Serving size = ½ cup

Oatmeal is the perfect morning meal to keep you going throughout the early part of your day. Full of fiber to keep you full and sweetened with honey, this cinnamon oatmeal is the ideal meal to wake up to.

2 cups water

1 teaspoon vanilla extract

1 cup rolled oats

1 cup unsweetened applesauce

1 tablespoon raw honey

1 teaspoon ground cinnamon

1. Place the rolled oats in a blender or food processor and pulse until the oats are finely ground.

2. Combine the water and vanilla extract in a small saucepan over medium-high heat and then whisk in the ground oats.

3. Bring the mixture to a boil; then reduce the heat and simmer it for about 3 minutes.

4. Stir in the unsweetened applesauce, honey, and ground cinnamon.

5. Simmer the mixture for about 1 minute longer; remove from heat.

6. Let sit for 2 or 3 minutes. Serve hot.

Per Serving Calories 56; Total fat: 1g; Saturated fat: 0g; Total carbs: 12g; Fiber: 1g; Cholesterol: 0mg; Protein: 1g

Raisin Apple Breakfast Oats

Makes About 3 Cups • Serving Size = about ½ Cup

If you don't like plain oatmeal, these raisin apple breakfast oats might make you reconsider. Full of raisins and sweet apple flavor, these breakfast oats will hit the spot.

1 cup rolled oats

2 cups water

1 teaspoon vanilla extract

1 cup unsweetened applesauce

1 medium apple, peeled, cored, and chopped

1 tablespoon pure maple syrup

1 teaspoon ground cinnamon

¼ cup raisins

1. Place the rolled oats in a blender or food processor and pulse until the oats are finely ground.

2. Combine the water and vanilla extract in a small saucepan over medium-high heat and then whisk in the ground oats.

3. Bring the mixture to a boil and then reduce the heat and simmer it for about 3 minutes.

4. Stir in the unsweetened applesauce, chopped apples, maple syrup, and ground cinnamon.

5. Simmer the mixture for about 1 minute longer and remove from heat.

6. Let sit for 2 or 3 minutes. Serve hot, garnished with raisins.

Per Serving Calories 83; Total fat: 1g; Saturated fat: 0g; Total carbs: 19g; Fiber: 2g; Cholesterol: 0mg; Protein: 1g

Strawberry Banana Overnight Oats

Serves 4 to 6 • Serving size = about ¾ cup

These oats are perfect for a quick breakfast. Simply combine the ingredients the night before and then store in the refrigerator and serve in the morning!

2 cups rolled oats

2 cups unsweetened almond milk

¼ cup pure maple syrup

2 small bananas, peeled and sliced

1¼ cups fresh strawberries, chopped

½ cup chopped pecans

2 tablespoons ground flaxseed

1 teaspoon ground cinnamon

1 teaspoon almond extract

Pinch of salt

1. Combine all of the ingredients in a large mixing bowl and stir well.

2. Spoon the mixture into a casserole dish; cover with plastic and refrigerate overnight.

3. Spoon into bowls in the morning and serve cold, topped with granola if desired.

Per Serving Calories 220; Total fat: 7g; Saturated fat: 1g; Total carbs: 39g; Fiber: 6g; Cholesterol: 0mg; Protein: 4g

Steel-Cut Oatmeal with Dried Cranberries

Serves 4 • Serving size = about ¾ cup

Steel-cut oats are full of the fiber your body needs to stay full and focused throughout the morning. Topped with dried cranberries, this oatmeal is sure to satisfy.

1 cup unsweetened almond milk

2 cups water

1 cup steel-cut oats

Pinch of salt

1 cup mashed banana

1 tablespoon ground flaxseed

1½ teaspoons ground cinnamon

1 teaspoon vanilla extract

½ cup raisins

¼ cup dried cranberries

1. Combine the almond milk and water in a medium saucepan and bring to a boil.

2. Stir in the oats and salt; then reduce the heat to low.

3. Whisk in the mashed banana and flaxseed; then simmer for about 20 minutes. Stir the oats every 5 to 6 minutes.

4. Remove from heat and stir in the remaining ingredients.

5. Serve immediately or portion out into containers and store in the refrigerator.

6. To reheat, add a tablespoon or so of almond milk and warm up in the microwave.

Per Serving Calories 162; Total fat: 2g; Saturated fat: 0g; Total carbs: 34g; Fiber: 5g; Cholesterol: 0mg; Protein: 3g

Chocolate Chip Pancakes

Makes about 8 medium pancakes • Serving size = about 2 medium pancakes

Chocolate chip pancakes are a treat that everyone in your family can enjoy, vegetarian or not. This recipe is incredibly easy to make, and you can store the leftover batter in the refrigerator to enjoy later in the week.

1 cup skim milk

2 tablespoons butter, melted

1 large egg, beaten

1 cup all-purpose flour

2 tablespoons granulated sugar

2 teaspoons baking powder

Pinch of salt

½ cup mini chocolate chips

1. Whisk together the milk, butter, and egg in a mixing bowl.

2. Whisk together the flour, sugar, baking powder, and salt in a separate bowl, and then add them to the milk mixture.

3. Heat a large nonstick skillet over medium heat.

4. Spoon the batter into the skillet, using 3 to 4 tablespoons per pancake.

5. Drop 1 to 2 teaspoons of mini chocolate chips into the wet batter for each pancake.

6. Cook the pancakes until bubbles form on the surface, and then carefully flip the pancakes using a plastic spatula.

7. Cook the pancakes until browned on the underside, about 1 minute more.

8. Transfer the pancakes to a plate and repeat with the remaining batter.

9. Serve hot, drizzled with maple syrup, if desired.

Per Serving Calories 240; Total fat: 8g; Saturated fat: 4g; Total carbs: 35g; Fiber: 1g; Cholesterol: 63mg; Protein: 7g

Almond Butter Pancakes

Makes about 6 medium pancakes • Serving size = about 2 medium pancakes

If you are in need of a recipe to break up your boring breakfast routine, try these almond butter pancakes. If you are feeling extra adventurous, try making your own almond butter by blending raw almonds in a food processor for several minutes until smooth.

1¼ cups whole-wheat flour

2 tablespoons cane sugar

2 teaspoons baking powder

Pinch of salt

2 tablespoons warm water

½ tablespoon Ener-G Egg Replacer

1⅓ cups unsweetened almond milk

2 tablespoons natural almond butter

2 tablespoons unsweetened applesauce

1. Whisk together the flour, sugar, baking powder, and salt in a mixing bowl.

2. In a small bowl, whisk together the warm water and egg replacer.

3. Whisk the almond milk into the dry ingredients and then whisk in the water and egg replacer mixture.

4. Add the almond butter and applesauce and then whisk the mixture until smooth.

5. Heat a large nonstick skillet over medium heat.

6. Spoon the batter into the skillet, using 3 to 4 tablespoons per pancake.

7. Cook the pancakes until bubbles form on the surface and then carefully flip the pancakes using a plastic spatula.

8. Cook the pancakes until browned on the underside, about 1 minute more.

9. Transfer the pancakes to a plate and repeat with the remaining batter.

10. Serve hot, drizzled with maple syrup, if desired.

Per Serving Calories 379; Total fat: 13g; Saturated fat: 2g; Total carbs: 58g; Fiber: 4g; Cholesterol: 0mg; Protein: 10g

Pumpkin Cinnamon Pancakes

Makes about 6 medium pancakes • Serving size = about 2 medium pancakes

These pumpkin cinnamon pancakes are the perfect treat to enjoy during the fall. If you are lucky enough to have a farmers' market nearby, purchase some fresh pumpkins to make your own purée for these pancakes.

1¼ cups whole-wheat flour

2 tablespoons cane sugar

2 teaspoons baking powder

1½ teaspoons ground cinnamon

Pinch of salt

1 cup unsweetened almond milk

1 large egg, beaten

1 cup pumpkin purée

1. Whisk together the flour, sugar, baking powder, cinnamon, and salt in a mixing bowl.

2. Whisk the almond milk into the dry ingredients, and then whisk in the beaten egg.

3. Add the pumpkin and whisk the mixture until smooth.

4. Heat a large nonstick skillet over medium heat.

5. Spoon the batter into the skillet, using 3 to 4 tablespoons per pancake.

6. Cook the pancakes until bubbles form on the surface, and then carefully flip the pancakes using a plastic spatula.

7. Cook the pancakes until browned on the underside, about 1 minute more.

8. Transfer the pancakes to a plate and repeat with the remaining batter.

9. Serve hot, drizzled with maple syrup, if desired.

Per Serving Calories 291; Total fat: 4g; Saturated fat: 1g; Total carbs: 58g; Fiber: 5g; Cholesterol: 62mg; Protein: 9g

Whole-Wheat Buttermilk Waffles

Makes about 8 waffles • Serving size = 1 waffle

If you love the flavor of buttermilk waffles but are looking for something a little bit healthier, try using whole-wheat flour! These whole-wheat buttermilk waffles turn out crisp on the outside but full of sweet, buttery flavor.

1 cup whole-wheat flour

3 tablespoons cane sugar

1 teaspoon baking powder

Pinch of salt

1 cup buttermilk

2 tablespoons butter, melted

1. Preheat waffle iron to high.

2. Whisk together the flour, sugar, baking powder, and salt in a mixing bowl.

3. Whisk in the buttermilk and melted butter, stirring until just combined.

4. Pour about ¼ cup of batter into the waffle iron and cook until crisp and lightly browned.

5. Repeat with the remaining waffles and serve hot.

Per Serving Calories 112; Total fat: 3g; Saturated fat: 2g; Total carbs: 18g; Fiber: 0g; Cholesterol: 9mg; Protein: 3g

Tomato Basil Omelet

Serves 1

This omelet is the perfect way to use fresh produce from your local farmers' market or from your own garden. Feel free to substitute whatever fresh herbs you have on hand!

2 eggs

1 tablespoon skim milk

Pinch of salt and pepper

2 teaspoons olive oil, divided

1 garlic clove, minced

1 small Roma tomato, diced

4 to 6 fresh basil leaves, chopped

1. Whisk together the eggs, milk, salt, and pepper in a small bowl, and then set aside.

2. Heat 1 teaspoon olive oil in a small frying pan over medium heat.

3. Add the garlic and cook for 1 minute.

4. Stir in the tomato and basil and cook until the basil is just wilted, about 2 minutes. Transfer the mixture to a bowl and set aside.

5. Heat the remaining 1 teaspoon of olive oil in the frying pan.

6. Pour the egg mixture into the pan and tilt the pan to coat the bottom with egg.

7. Cook the eggs for about 1 minute; then use a plastic spatula to scrape down the sides of the pan, letting the uncooked egg spread.

8. Let the egg cook for 1 to 2 minutes more until it is almost set.

9. Spoon the garlic, tomato, and basil mixture over half of the omelet and fold the empty half over top of the filling.

10. Cook the omelet for 1 to 2 minutes more until the egg is set.

11. Slide the omelet onto a plate to serve.

Per Serving Calories 256; Total fat: 18g; Saturated fat: 4g; Total carbs: 12g; Fiber: 2g; Cholesterol: 328mg; Protein: 14g

Spinach and Blue Cheese Omelet

Serves 1

If you are looking for a unique and satisfying breakfast recipe, this omelet is it. Made with fresh spinach, eggs, and blue cheese, it's sure to hit the spot.

2 eggs

1 tablespoon skim milk

Pinch of salt and pepper

2 teaspoons olive oil, divided

1 garlic clove, minced

¼ cup vidalia onion, thinly sliced

1 cup fresh baby spinach

2 tablespoons blue cheese crumbles

1. Whisk together the eggs, milk, salt, and pepper in a small bowl; set aside.

2. Heat 1 teaspoon of olive oil in a small frying pan over medium heat.

3. Add the garlic and onion, and then cook for 1 minute.

4. Stir in the baby spinach and cook until it is just wilted, about 2 minutes.

5. Transfer the garlic, onion, and spinach mixture to a bowl and set aside.

6. Heat the remaining 1 teaspoon of olive oil in the frying pan.

7. Pour the egg mixture into the pan and tilt the pan to coat the bottom with egg.

8. Cook the eggs for about 1 minute and then use a plastic spatula to scrape down the sides of the pan, letting the uncooked egg spread.

9. Let the egg cook for 1 to 2 minutes more until it is almost set.

10. Spoon the garlic, onion, and spinach mixture over half of the omelet and sprinkle the blue cheese crumbles over that.

11. Fold the empty half over top of the filling.

12. Cook the omelet for 1 to 2 minutes more until the egg is set.

13. Carefully slide the omelet onto a plate to serve.

Per Serving Calories 301; Total fat: 23g; Saturated fat: 7g; Total carbs: 7g; Fiber: 1g; Cholesterol: 385mg; Protein: 18g

NINE

Soups, Salads, and Dressings

Though salads are sometimes referred to as "rabbit food" and are assumed to be the staple of the vegetarian diet, they do not have to be boring! A salad is the perfect opportunity to combine the flavors of a variety of crisp vegetables—you can also enhance your salads by topping them with fresh fruit, nuts, or seeds. Vegetarian soups are just as versatile, and they can be served cold to cool you down on a hot summer day or hot to warm you up during the winter. In this chapter you will find a selection of unique soups, salads, and dressings for any occasion.

RECIPES

Black Bean and Corn Salsa

Serves about 6 • Serving size = about 1 cup

This black bean and corn salsa is something you can whip up in just a few minutes. It's the perfect side dish for a Mexican meal or an appetizer for a friendly get-together.

Two 15-ounce cans black beans

2½ cups frozen corn, thawed

1 medium ripe tomato, diced

½ small red onion, thinly sliced

½ cup fresh cilantro leaves, chopped

¼ cup fresh lemon juice

1 tablespoon fresh lime juice

2 teaspoons honey

½ teaspoon sea salt

¼ teaspoon freshly ground black pepper

1. Rinse the beans well under fresh water.

2. Drain the beans and place them in a large serving bowl.

3. Add the corn, tomato, red onion, and cilantro. Toss well to combine.

4. For the dressing: Whisk together the remaining ingredients in a small bowl.

5. Drizzle the dressing over the salad and toss to coat. Serve immediately.

Per Serving Calories 160; Total fat: 2g; Saturated fat: 0g; Total carbs: 33g; Fiber: 7g; Cholesterol: 0mg; Protein: 7g

Gazpacho

Serves 4 • Serving size = about 1 cup

Gazpacho is a cold, summer soup from Spain that combines the flavors of your favorite summer vegetables. Take advantage of your local farmers' market or produce grown in your garden at home to make this fresh and flavorful gazpacho.

6 ripe Roma tomatoes, halved

1 sweet red pepper, seeded and chopped

1 green bell pepper, seeded and chopped

1 small red onion, quartered

1 garlic clove, peeled and sliced

3 cups organic tomato juice

¼ cup white wine vinegar

¼ cup extra-virgin olive oil

½ teaspoon salt

¼ teaspoon fresh ground black pepper

1. Place the tomatoes in a food processor and pulse until finely chopped but not puréed.

2. Transfer the tomatoes to a bowl.

3. Place the red and green peppers in a food processor and pulse until finely chopped.

4. Transfer the peppers to the bowl with the tomatoes, and place the onion and garlic in the food processor.

5. Pulse the onion and garlic until finely chopped and add to the bowl with the vegetables.

6. Stir in the tomato juice, vinegar, olive oil, salt, and pepper.

7. Cover the bowl and chill overnight; serve cold.

Per Serving Calories 219; Total fat: 13g; Saturated fat: 2g; Total carbs: 25g; Fiber: 5g; Cholesterol: 0mg; Protein: 5g

Chilled Watermelon Gazpacho

Serves 4 to 6 • Serving size = about 1 cup

A twist on traditional tomato gazpacho, this chilled watermelon version is both sweet and satisfying.

6 cups seedless watermelon, chopped

2 large seedless cucumbers, diced

2 scallions, chopped

½ cup rice wine vinegar

¼ cup fresh cilantro leaves

1 tablespoon olive oil

3 tablespoons fresh mint leaves

1. Combine all of the ingredients in a large mixing bowl.

2. Stir well to combine and then cover and chill for 2 hours.

3. Mash the watermelon using the back of a wooden spoon and serve cold.

Per Serving Calories 146; Total fat: 4g; Saturated fat: 1g; Total carbs: 24g; Fiber: 2g; Cholesterol: 0mg; Protein: 3g

Chilled Avocado Soup

Serves 6 • Serving size = about 1 cup

Cool and creamy, this chilled avocado soup is just what you need to cool down on a hot summer day.

3 ripe avocados, pitted and chopped

2 cups vegetable stock

½ cup minced red onion

¼ cup fresh chopped cilantro leaves

2 tablespoons fresh lemon juice

1 teaspoon salt

1 cup whole milk

1. Combine the avocado, vegetable stock, red onion, cilantro, lemon juice, and salt in a food processor.

2. Blend the mixture until smooth and then pour into a serving bowl.

3. Cover and chill for several hours until cold.

4. Whisk in the whole milk just before serving and garnish with cilantro leaves.

Per Serving Calories 236; Total fat: 21g; Saturated fat: 5g; Total carbs: 12g; Fiber: 7g; Cholesterol: 4mg; Protein: 3g

Tomato Basil Bisque

Serves 4 to 6 • Serving size = about 1 cup

Tomatoes are an excellent source of vitamin C, and they also contain high levels of copper, iron, magnesium, and potassium. Tomatoes also contain lycopene, an antioxidant that has been linked to cancer prevention.

2½ pounds ripe tomatoes

2 yellow onions, thinly sliced

2 tablespoons minced garlic

1 cup chopped basil leaves

3 tablespoons olive oil

Salt and pepper

1 cup vegetable stock

½ cup heavy cream

1. Preheat oven to 450°F.

2. Rinse the tomatoes in cool water and then cut them in half.

3. Spread the tomatoes on a rimmed baking sheet and sprinkle the onions, garlic, and chopped basil over the top of them.

4. Drizzle with olive oil and season with salt and pepper.

5. Roast the vegetables for 20 to 25 minutes, or until the onions are caramelized and the tomatoes slightly charred.

6. Scoop the vegetables into a large stockpot.

7. Add the vegetable stock and bring the mixture to a boil.

8. Remove from heat and purée the soup using an immersion blender.

9. Whisk in the heavy cream in a steady stream and return the soup to the heat.

10. Cook until heated through.

11. Serve hot, garnished with fresh basil leaves.

Per Serving Calories 225; Total fat: 17g; Saturated fat: 6g; Total carbs: 19g; Fiber: 5g; Cholesterol: 21mg; Protein: 4g

Kale and Mushroom Soup

Serves 6 • Serving size = about 1 cup

The perfect combination of mushrooms and wilted greens, this kale and mushroom soup is sure to hit the spot.

1 tablespoon coconut oil

1 teaspoon minced garlic

2 pounds fresh mushrooms, chopped

1 large yellow onion, chopped

5 cups low-sodium vegetable broth, divided

3 cups chopped curly kale

½ teaspoon salt

¼ teaspoon freshly ground black pepper

1. Heat the oil in a stockpot over medium-high heat.

2. Add the garlic and cook for 1 minute.

3. Stir in the mushrooms and onion and cook for 6 to 8 minutes until tender.

4. Add the vegetable broth and bring to a boil.

5. Reduce heat and simmer for 20 minutes.

6. Stir in the kale, salt, and pepper.

7. Cook for 2 to 3 minutes until the kale is wilted and serve hot.

Per Serving Calories 92; Total fat: 3g; Saturated fat: 2g; Total carbs: 12g; Fiber: 3g; Cholesterol: 0mg; Protein: 8g

Roasted Leek and Sweet Potato Soup

Serves 6 • Serving size = about 1 cup

Sweet potatoes are an excellent source of iron, copper, and magnesium. They are beneficial for eye health and have also been shown to improve digestion and to support detoxification.

2 pounds sweet potatoes, quartered

2 leeks, rinsed and chopped (white and light-green parts only)

3 tablespoons olive oil, divided

1 tablespoon minced garlic

1 large yellow onion, chopped

5 cups low-sodium vegetable broth

1 teaspoon salt

½ teaspoon freshly ground black pepper

1 cup unsweetened coconut milk

1. Preheat oven to 375°F.

2. Place the potatoes and leeks in a large bowl.

3. Add 2 tablespoons olive oil and the garlic and toss to coat.

4. Spread the potatoes and leeks on a rimmed baking sheet and roast for 30 to 40 minutes, until lightly charred.

5. Heat the remaining tablespoon olive oil in a stockpot over medium heat.

6. Stir in the onions and cook until tender, about 5 minutes.

7. Add the roasted potatoes and leeks and stir well.

8. Stir in the vegetable broth, salt, and pepper.

9. Bring the soup to a boil; then remove from heat and purée using an immersion blender.

10. Whisk in the coconut milk and serve hot.

Per Serving Calories 312; Total fat: 17g; Saturated fat: 10g; Total carbs: 37g; Fiber: 7g; Cholesterol: 0mg; Protein: 6g

Lentil Soup

Lentils are a good source of both dietary fiber and protein. In this recipe, they combine well with onions and tomatoes, flavored with garlic and ground cumin.

1 pound dry lentils

2 tablespoons olive oil

1 teaspoon minced garlic

1 yellow onion, chopped

1 large celery stalk, chopped

1 teaspoon salt

¼ teaspoon black pepper

1 cup chopped tomatoes

8 cups low-sodium vegetable broth

½ teaspoon ground cumin

1. Rinse the lentils in fresh water; drain and set aside.

2. Heat the olive oil in a stockpot over medium heat.

3. Add the garlic and cook for 1 minute.

4. Stir in the onion and celery, season with salt and pepper, and cook until tender, about 6 to 8 minutes.

5. Add the lentils, tomatoes, vegetable broth, and ground cumin and bring the soup to a boil.

6. Reduce heat and simmer the soup, covered, for 35 to 40 minutes.

7. Remove the soup from heat and purée using an immersion blender; serve hot.

Per Serving Calories 343; Total fat: 6g; Saturated fat: 1g; Total carbs: 50g; Fiber: 24g; Cholesterol: 0mg; Protein: 23g

Cream of Asparagus Soup

Asparagus contains high levels of folate and antioxidants, which have been shown to reduce the signs of aging and to slow cognitive decline. It also contains vitamins A, C, and E, as well as chromium and dietary fiber.

2 pounds fresh asparagus spears

8 cups water

3 tablespoons olive oil

3 tablespoons rice flour

1 yellow onion, diced

1 teaspoon minced garlic

1 cup chopped leeks, white and light-green parts only

Salt and pepper

1. Rinse the asparagus spears in water; trim off the ends and chop the asparagus into ½-inch chunks.

2. Bring the water to boil in a large stockpot and add the chopped asparagus.

3. Boil the asparagus for 3 minutes; drain, reserving the liquid.

4. Heat the olive oil in a large saucepan over medium-high heat.

5. Whisk in the flour to form a roux and then stir in the onion, garlic, and chopped leeks.

6. Cook the mixture, stirring often, for 5 minutes until the onion begins to soften.

7. Stir in the chopped asparagus and the reserved cooking liquid; bring the mixture to a simmer.

8. Simmer the soup, covered, for about 25 minutes until the asparagus is tender.

9. Remove the soup from the heat and purée using an immersion blender.

→

10. Strain the soup through a mesh sieve and discard the solids.

11. Pour the soup back into the saucepan and whisk in the salt and pepper.

12. Cover the soup and chill for 4 to 6 hours, until cold, before serving.

13. Garnish each serving with a sprig of fresh parsley or cilantro.

Per Serving Calories 188; Total fat: 11g; Saturated fat: 2g; Total carbs: 21g; Fiber: 6g; Cholesterol: 0mg; Protein: 6g

Creamy Cauliflower Soup

Serves 4 • Serving size = about 1 cup

Cauliflower is known for its high nutrient content. Loaded with B vitamins, potassium, manganese, and more, it is one of the most nutrient-dense vegetables out there. It is also a great source of anti-oxidants, which help to support the liver's detox abilities.

1 tablespoon coconut oil

1 teaspoon minced garlic

1 small onion, chopped

1 large celery stalk, chopped

½ teaspoon salt

¼ teaspoon black pepper

4 cups low-sodium vegetable broth

1 head cauliflower, chopped

1. Heat the coconut oil in a large saucepan over medium heat.

2. Stir in the garlic and cook for 1 minute.

3. Add the onion and celery and cook for 6 to 8 minutes until softened.

4. Stir in the salt, pepper, and vegetable broth.

5. Add the cauliflower and then bring the soup to a boil.

6. Reduce heat and simmer for 20 to 25 minutes until the cauliflower is tender.

7. Remove from heat and purée the soup using an immersion blender.

8. Cool the soup to room temperature; then cover and chill for 2 to 4 hours. Serve cold.

Per Serving Calories 95; Total fat: 4g; Saturated fat: 3g; Total carbs: 12g; Fiber: 5g; Cholesterol: 0mg; Protein: 5g

Curried Butternut Squash Stew

Serves 4 • Serving size = about 1 cup

This butternut squash stew is full of flavor—raisins, crushed tomatoes, and curry powder all work together with the fresh butternut squash to create a truly unique and delicious dish.

1 medium butternut squash

2 tablespoons coconut oil

1 teaspoon minced garlic

1 yellow onion, chopped

One 14-ounce can chickpeas, rinsed and drained

One 14-ounce can crushed tomatoes

3 cups low-sodium vegetable broth

½ cup golden raisins

1 teaspoon curry powder

Salt and freshly ground pepper

1. Cut the butternut squash in half using a sharp knife.

2. Peel the squash using a sharp knife and scoop out the seeds.

3. Chop the squash into 1-inch cubes.

4. Heat the oil in a Dutch oven over medium-high heat.

5. Add the garlic and cook for 1 minute.

6. Stir in the onion and cook for 5 to 7 minutes until softened.

7. Stir in the chickpeas, tomatoes, and vegetable broth.

8. Bring the stew to a boil and then reduce heat to low.

9. Stir in the raisins, curry powder, salt, and pepper and simmer for 1 to 2 hours until the squash is tender.

10. Serve the stew hot.

Per Serving Calories 345; Total fat: 9g; Saturated fat: 6g; Total carbs: 60g; Fiber: 12g; Cholesterol: 0mg; Protein: 12g

Sweet Potato Stew

Serves 6 • Serving size = about 1 cup

This sweet potato stew is hot and hearty, just what you need to fill you up on a chilly day. Made with carrots, celery, and sweet potato, this recipe is full of nutritious and delicious flavor.

2 tablespoons coconut oil

1 teaspoon minced garlic

1 yellow onion, quartered

2 large carrots, chopped

2 large celery stalks, chopped

2 pounds sweet potato, peeled and roughly chopped

2 cups low-sodium vegetable stock

1½ teaspoons dried oregano

1 teaspoon salt

½ teaspoon freshly ground pepper

1. Heat the coconut oil in a heavy skillet over medium-high heat.

2. Add the garlic and cook for 1 minute.

3. Stir in the onion, carrots, and celery and cook for 4 minutes.

4. Stir in the sweet potato and cook for 5 minutes more.

5. Transfer the vegetables to a slow cooker.

6. Whisk together the remaining ingredients and pour over the ingredients in the slow cooker.

7. Cover the slow cooker and cook on low heat for 4 to 6 hours. Serve hot.

Per Serving Calories 188; Total fat: 5g; Saturated fat: 4g; Total carbs: 34g; Fiber: 7g; Cholesterol: 0mg; Protein: 3g

Red Bean Chili

Serves 6 • Serving size = about 1 cup

If you are looking for a hearty, mouthwatering meal, look no further than this red bean chili. This recipe is proof that you can still have a delicious, satisfying meal without any meat at all.

2 cups dried red beans, rinsed well

8 cups water

¼ cup olive oil

1 tablespoon minced garlic

1 large onion, chopped

2 large carrots, chopped

1 small zucchini, diced

1 tablespoon chili powder

½ teaspoon salt

1. Place the beans and water in a stockpot and bring it to a boil.

2. Reduce the heat to low and simmer the beans, covered, for 45 to 55 minutes until the beans are tender.

3. Remove the stockpot from heat.

4. Heat the olive oil in a Dutch oven over medium-high heat.

5. Add the garlic and cook for 1 minute.

6. Stir in the onion and carrots and cook for 5 to 8 minutes.

7. Stir in the remaining ingredients and simmer for 10 to 12 minutes.

Per Serving Calories 308; Total fat: 9g; Saturated fat: 1g; Total carbs: 44g; Fiber: 11g; Cholesterol: 0mg; Protein: 15g

Broccoli Salad with Almonds

Serves about 8 • Serving size = about 1 cup

Broccoli contains a wealth of vitamins and minerals, including vitamin E, potassium, calcium, and selenium. In this recipe the crispness of fresh broccoli pairs delightfully with the crunch of sliced almonds and diced carrot.

6 cups fresh broccoli florets, chopped

1 large celery stalk, diced

1 peeled carrot, diced

dressing

⅓ cup sesame tahini

3 tablespoons raw honey

1 tablespoon extra-virgin olive oil

1 tablespoon fresh lemon juice

½ cup thinly sliced almonds

¼ cup thinly sliced scallions

1. Combine the broccoli, celery, and carrots in a bowl. Stir well.

2. To make the dressing: Place the tahini, honey, olive oil, and lemon juice in a bowl and whisk until smooth and combined.

3. Pour the dressing over the salad and toss to coat.

4. Toss with the scallions and sliced almonds just before serving.

Per Serving Calories 229; Total fat: 18g; Saturated fat: 2g; Total carbs: 16g; Fiber: 6g; Cholesterol: 0mg; Protein: 8g

Sun-dried Tomato Spinach Salad

Serves 2

Spinach is loaded with a variety of different vitamins and minerals, including vitamins A, C, E, calcium, iron, and potassium; it is also a good source of vegetarian protein. This salad is the best of both worlds—high in nutrients as well as flavor.

4 cups baby
spinach leaves

2 cups chopped
romaine lettuce

1 cup cherry
tomatoes, halved

¼ cup thinly sliced red
onion dressing

2 sun-dried tomatoes
in oil, drained

2 tablespoons
extra-virgin olive oil

2 tablespoons
balsamic vinegar

1 teaspoon minced garlic

Freshly ground
black pepper

1. Rinse the spinach and romaine in fresh water and drain well.

2. Add the cherry tomatoes and red onion; toss well.

3. Combine the remaining ingredients in a food processor.

4. To make the dressing: Pulse the dressing ingredients twice and then blend until smooth and well combined.

5. Drizzle the dressing over the salad and toss to coat.

6. Divide the salad between two bowls.

7. Garnish with pepper to serve.

Per Serving Calories 175; Total fat: 15g; Saturated fat: 2g; Total carbs: 10g; Fiber: 3g; Cholesterol: 0mg; Protein: 3g

Mandarin Spinach Salad with Walnuts

Serves 2

Mandarin oranges are known for their sweet flavor as well as their high vitamin C content. In this recipe, the oranges provide a great balance to the crunch of chopped walnuts and the crispness of fresh spinach.

4 cups fresh baby spinach

1 small can mandarin oranges, drained

¼ small red onion, thinly sliced

¼ cup chopped walnuts

1. Combine the spinach, oranges, and red onion in a salad bowl.

2. Toss the salad to combine the ingredients and then divide between two bowls.

3. Top each salad with sliced walnuts to serve.

Per Serving Calories 88; Total fat: 3g; Saturated fat: 0g; Total carbs: 15g; Fiber: 3g; Cholesterol: 0mg; Protein: 3g

Chopped Tomato and Avocado Salad

Serves 4 • Serving size = about ½ cup

Avocados are a great natural source of heart-healthy monounsaturated fats. They also contain potassium, which helps regulate blood pressure. Combined with the cancer-fighting lycopene of fresh tomatoes, this recipe packs a powerful punch.

2 cups frozen corn, thawed

2 ripe plum tomatoes, diced

1 ripe avocado, pitted and diced

¼ cup fresh chopped cilantro leaves

2 tablespoons lime juice

Salt and pepper

1. Combine the corn, tomatoes, and avocado in a mixing bowl.

2. Add the remaining ingredients and toss to coat.

3. Chill the salad for at least 1 hour before serving.

Per Serving Calories 180; Total fat: 11g; Saturated fat: 2g; Total carbs: 22g; Fiber: 6g; Cholesterol: 0mg; Protein: 4g

Chopped Salad with Avocado

serves about 6 • serving size = about 1½ cups

This chopped salad is the perfect combination of fresh vegetables and avocado. Tossed in a lemon lime dressing, this salad is incredibly refreshing.

4 cups chopped romaine lettuce

1 cup cherry tomatoes, halved

1 sweet orange pepper, chopped

½ small red onion, chopped

3 tablespoons fresh lime juice

3 tablespoons fresh lemon juice

2 tablespoons extra-virgin olive oil

½ teaspoon sea salt

¼ teaspoon ground cumin

1 ripe avocado, peeled, pitted, and chopped

Freshly ground black pepper

1. Combine the chopped lettuce, tomatoes, orange pepper, and red onion in a bowl and toss well.

2. To make the dressing: Whisk together the lime juice, lemon juice, olive oil, sea salt, and cumin in a small bowl.

3. Add the dressing to the salad and toss to coat.

4. Spread the avocado on top of the salad.

5. Serve with freshly ground black pepper.

Per Serving Calories 129; Total fat: 11g; Saturated fat: 2g; Total carbs: 7g; Fiber: 3g; Cholesterol: 0mg; Protein: 1g

Strawberry Pecan Spring Salad

Serves 1

The perfect summer salad, this recipe combines the tenderness of spring greens with the crunch of pecans and the sweetness of fresh strawberries.

2 cups fresh spring greens

4 fresh strawberries, sliced

½ cup thinly sliced red cabbage

4 thin slices red onion

2 tablespoons chopped pecans

1. Rinse the spring greens in fresh water; drain well.

2. Transfer the greens to a bowl and toss with the strawberries and red cabbage.

3. Top the salad with the four slices of red onion and sprinkle with chopped pecans.

4. Serve immediately with your favorite dressing.

Per Serving Calories 81; Total fat: 3g; Saturated fat: 0g; Total carbs: 15g; Fiber: 4g; Cholesterol: 0mg; Protein: 2g

Quinoa Salad with Lentils and Tomatoes

Serves 4 • Serving size = about 1 cup

Quinoa is sometimes referred to as a "super grain" because it is packed with nutrients. Not only is it a good source of dietary fiber, but it also has a high protein content.

½ cup dried quinoa

2 cups water, divided

½ cup dried red lentils
dressing

3 tablespoons
extra-virgin olive oil

2 tablespoons red wine
vinegar

1 tablespoon fresh
lemon juice

3 tablespoons fresh
chopped cilantro

4 cups chopped
romaine lettuce

2 Roma tomatoes,
quartered

¼ cup thinly sliced
scallions

1. Place the quinoa in a mesh sieve and run under cold water for 2 minutes, swishing the quinoa with your hand.

2. Transfer the quinoa to a small saucepan and add 1 cup of water.

3. Bring the quinoa to a boil and then reduce heat and simmer for 15 minutes, until the quinoa absorbs the water. Remove from heat to cool.

4. Rinse the lentils under fresh water and place them in a medium saucepan with 2 cups of water.

5. Bring the lentils to a boil and then reduce heat and simmer for 30 minutes, covered. Drain the lentils and set aside to cool.

6. To make the dressing: Whisk together the olive oil, vinegar, lemon juice, and cilantro in a small bowl.

7. Combine the cooled quinoa and lentils in a serving bowl with the chopped romaine lettuce and tomatoes.

8. Toss the salad to coat with dressing; chill for 20 minutes. Garnish with scallions to serve.

Per Serving Calories 265; Total fat: 12g; Saturated fat: 2g; Total carbs: 30g; Fiber: 9g; Cholesterol: 0mg; Protein: 10g

Lemon Orzo Salad with Parsley

Serves about 8 • Serving size = about ¾ cup

If you are looking for a refreshing side dish or salad, this is the perfect recipe. Made with orzo pasta and tossed with diced cucumber, red onion, and a lemon vinaigrette, this salad is sure to satisfy.

2 cups orzo pasta

¼ cup extra-virgin olive oil

¼ cup fresh lemon juice

2 tablespoons apple cider vinegar

1 tablespoon lemon zest

1 cup cherry tomatoes, halved

1 celery stalk, diced

½ small red onion, diced

½ seedless cucumber, diced

½ cup fresh parsley leaves, chopped

Sea salt and freshly ground pepper

1. Bring a pot of water to boil and add the orzo.

2. Cook the orzo until it is tender, about 8 to 10 minutes, stirring occasionally.

3. Drain the orzo and then rinse in cool water and set aside in a large bowl.

4. For the dressing: Whisk together the olive oil, lemon juice, vinegar, and lemon zest in a small bowl.

5. Stir the tomatoes, celery, red onion, cucumber, and parsley into the bowl with the orzo.

6. Stir in the olive oil mixture and toss to coat. Season with salt and pepper; serve immediately.

Per Serving Calories 145; Total fat: 7g; Saturated fat: 1g; Total carbs: 18g; Fiber: 1g; Cholesterol: 0mg; Protein: 3g

Sweet Apple Dressing

Makes about 1 cup • Serving size = about 2 tablespoons

If you are looking for a sweet summer dressing, this sweet apple dressing is just what you need. Made with organic apple cider and apple cider vinegar, this dressing works well with summer salads topped with fresh fruit.

½ cup extra-virgin olive oil

⅓ cup organic apple cider

4 teaspoons apple cider vinegar

1 tablespoon minced white onion

Pinch of freshly ground pepper

1. Combine all of the ingredients in a small bowl.

2. Whisk until smooth and combined.

3. Chill the dressing until ready to serve.

Per Serving Calories 114; Total fat: 13g; Saturated fat: 2g; Total carbs: 1g; Fiber: 0g; Cholesterol: 0mg; Protein: 0g

Strawberry Poppy Seed Dressing

Makes about 1 cup • Serving size = about 2 tablespoons

This strawberry poppy seed dressing is the perfect way to dress up your summer salads. Made with fresh berries and dotted with poppy seeds, what more could you ask for?

½ cup fresh strawberries, chopped

⅓ cup extra-virgin olive oil

3 tablespoons raw honey

1 tablespoon balsamic vinegar

1 tablespoon fresh lemon juice

Pinch of salt and pepper

1 tablespoon poppy seeds

1. Combine all of the ingredients in a blender.

2. Blend the mixture until smooth and combined.

3. Chill until ready to use.

Per Serving Calories 106; Total fat: 9g; Saturated fat: 1g; Total carbs: 8g; Fiber: 0g; Cholesterol: 0mg; Protein: 0g

Lemon Lime Dressing

Makes about ¾ cup • Serving size = about 2 tablespoons

This lemon lime dressing has a light, citrusy flavor that goes well with virtually any summer salad. Drizzle it over fresh greens or use it as a marinade for grilled vegetables.

1½ tablespoons lemon juice

1 tablespoon lime juice

1 teaspoon fresh lemon zest

Pinch of dry mustard powder

¼ cup extra-virgin olive oil

¼ cup grapeseed oil

1. Whisk together the lemon juice, lime juice, lemon zest, and mustard powder in a bowl.

2. While whisking the mixture, drizzle in the olive oil and then the grapeseed oil.

3. Chill until ready to serve.

Per Serving Calories 109; Total fat: 12g; Saturated fat: 1g; Total carbs: 0g; Fiber: 0g; Cholesterol: 0mg; Protein: 0g

Sesame Lime Dressing

Makes about ¾ cup • Serving size = about 2 tablespoons

If you are looking for a unique and flavorful dressing for your favorite salads, look no further than this sesame lime dressing. Made with sesame tahini and fresh lime juice, this dressing is full of authentic flavor.

¼ cup tahini sauce

2 tablespoons fresh lime juice

Pinch of salt and pepper

¼ cup extra-virgin olive oil

1 tablespoon toasted sesame seeds

1. Combine the tahini, lime juice, salt, and pepper in a bowl.

2. Whisk the ingredients until smooth and combined.

3. While whisking, drizzle in the olive oil.

4. Add the sesame seeds and stir until well combined.

Per Serving Calories 139; Total fat: 14g; Saturated fat: 2g; Total carbs: 4g; Fiber: 1g; Cholesterol: 0mg; Protein: 2g

French-Style Dressing

Makes about 1½ cups • Serving size = about 2 tablespoons

This French-style dressing pairs well with fresh greens and crisp vegetables. Drizzle it over your favorite salad or use it as a dip for chopped veggies.

½ cup extra-virgin olive oil

½ cup vegan ketchup

¼ cup white wine vinegar

¼ cup cane sugar

2 tablespoons dried onion

1 teaspoon garlic powder

Pinch of salt and pepper

1. Combine all of the ingredients in a blender.

2. Blend the mixture until smooth and combined.

3. Chill until ready to use.

Per Serving Calories 101; Total fat: 8g; Saturated fat: 1g; Total carbs: 7g; Fiber: 0g; Cholesterol: 0mg; Protein: 0g

Traditional Italian Dressing

Makes about 1 cup • Serving size = about 2 tablespoons

This traditional Italian dressing is incredibly versatile—not only can you use it as a dressing for fresh salads, but you can also use it to marinate vegetables before roasting or grilling them.

1 tablespoon red wine vinegar

2 tablespoons white wine vinegar

½ teaspoon dried oregano

½ teaspoon dried parsley

½ teaspoon dried basil

½ teaspoon salt

¼ teaspoon freshly ground pepper

¾ cup extra-virgin olive oil

1. Whisk together the vinegars and spices in a bowl.

2. Pour the mixture into a food processor and pulse to blend.

3. With the food processor running, drizzle in the olive oil until well combined.

Per Serving Calories 164; Total fat: 19g; Saturated fat: 3g; Total carbs: 0g; Fiber: 0g; Cholesterol: 0mg; Protein: 0g

Caesar Dressing

Makes about ¾ cup • Serving size = about 2 tablespoons

This cool and creamy dressing is the perfect blend of garlic and Parmesan cheese, ideal for dressing chopped romaine for a crisp Caesar salad.

2 teaspoons minced garlic

2 tablespoons grated Parmesan cheese

1 tablespoon mustard

1 tablespoon distilled white vinegar

1 tablespoon fresh lemon juice

Pinch of salt and pepper

½ cup extra-virgin olive oil

1. Place the garlic, Parmesan cheese, mustard, vinegar, lemon juice, salt, and pepper in a food processor.

2. Blend the mixture until smooth.

3. With the food processor running, pour in the olive oil.

4. Pour the dressing into a bowl; cover and chill until ready to serve.

Per Serving Calories 163; Total fat: 18g; Saturated fat: 3g; Total carbs: 1g; Fiber: 0g; Cholesterol: 2mg; Protein: 1g

Sweet and Sour Vinaigrette

Makes about ¾ cup • Serving size = about 2 tablespoons

This sweet and sour vinaigrette works equally well as a salad dressing and as a dip for fresh cut veggies. Drizzle it over a salad or serve it on the side with a veggie tray.

⅓ cup extra-virgin olive oil

2 tablespoons rice wine vinegar

2 tablespoons plum sauce

Pinch of salt and pepper

1. Combine all of the ingredients in a blender.

2. Blend the mixture until smooth and combined.

3. Chill until ready to use.

Per Serving Calories 111; Total fat: 11g; Saturated fat: 2g; Total carbs: 3g; Fiber: 0g; Cholesterol: 0mg; Protein: 0g

Raspberry Vinaigrette

Makes about ½ cup • Serving size = about 2 tablespoons

This vinaigrette is made with raspberry vinegar and dried basil to create a unique and flavorful dressing for crisp salads or grilled veggies.

¼ cup extra-virgin olive oil

2 teaspoons raspberry vinegar

2 teaspoons cane sugar

2 teaspoons dried basil

1 teaspoon garlic powder

¼ teaspoon dry mustard powder

Pinch of salt and black pepper

1. Combine all of the ingredients in a small bowl.

2. Whisk until smooth and combined.

3. Chill the dressing until ready to serve.

Per Serving Calories 119; Total fat: 13g; Saturated fat: 2g; Total carbs: 3g; Fiber: 0g; Cholesterol: 0mg; Protein: 0g

TEN

Quick and Easy Condiments

Any simple meal can be made special with the right condiments. In this chapter, you will find an assortment of flavorful condiments that are incredibly easy to make. Dress up a grilled vegetable sandwich with some Basil Pine Nut Pesto or drizzle steamed veggies with some fresh Hollandaise Sauce. These condiments are versatile enough to be used in a variety of ways, so don't be afraid to get creative!

RECIPES

Honey Almond Butter

Makes about 1 cup • Serving size = about 2 tablespoons

A delicious alternative to peanut butter, almond butter can be used in a variety of different ways. Use it as a dip for apple slices or swirl it into chocolate brownies—the options are endless!

1 cup raw almonds

1 teaspoon raw honey

Pinch of salt

1. Place the almonds in a food processor and pulse to finely chop.

2. Leave the food processor running for several minutes at a time, scraping down the sides of the bowl as needed.

3. After 10 minutes or so, the almonds should begin to turn smooth.

4. Add the honey and salt and continue to blend until the mixture is smooth and creamy.

Per Serving Calories 105; Total fat: 9g; Saturated fat: 1g; Total carbs: 5g; Fiber: 2g; Cholesterol: 0mg; Protein: 4g

Dill Sauce

Makes about 2 cups • Serving size = about 2 tablespoons

Made with fresh dill, this sauce is full of flavor. Use it as a dip for fresh veggies, or spread it on sandwiches or tacos for a burst of refreshing flavor.

2 cups light sour cream

1 teaspoon dijon mustard

2 tablespoons fresh chopped dill

1 tablespoon fresh lemon juice

1 teaspoon capers

½ teaspoon salt

¼ teaspoon ground white pepper

1. Whisk together all of the ingredients in a mixing bowl.

2. Cover the bowl and chill for at least 1 hour to let the flavors mesh.

Per Serving Calories 52; Total fat: 3g; Saturated fat: 0g; Total carbs: 4g; Fiber: 0g; Cholesterol: 12mg; Protein: 2g

Horseradish Sauce

Makes about 2½ cups • Serving size = about 2 tablespoons

This horseradish sauce is cool and creamy with a delightful kick. Feel free to increase or reduce the amount of horseradish to accommodate your tastes.

2 cups light sour cream

⅓ cup fresh grated horseradish

2 tablespoons fresh lemon juice

¾ teaspoon salt

Pinch black pepper

1. Whisk together all of the ingredients in a mixing bowl.

2. Cover and chill for at least 1 hour to combine the flavors.

3. Serve cold.

Per Serving Calories 42; Total fat: 3g; Saturated fat: 0g; Total carbs: 3g; Fiber: 0g; Cholesterol: 9mg; Protein: 2g

Hollandaise Sauce

Makes about 1½ cups • Serving size = about 2 tablespoons

This hollandaise sauce is creamy and full of flavor—it is perfect for drizzling over steamed veggies.

3 egg yolks

1 tablespoon fresh lemon juice

1 stick unsalted butter

½ cup dry white wine

1 bay leaf

4 whole peppercorns

1 tablespoon distilled white vinegar

Pinch of salt

1. Combine the egg yolks and lemon juice in a medium saucepan over low heat.

2. Stir in the butter and white wine, whisking until the butter is melted.

3. Add the remaining ingredients and stir until the sauce has thickened (do not let it get hot too fast or the eggs will curdle the sauce).

4. Remove the bay leaf and keep the sauce warm in a double boiler until ready to use.

Per Serving Calories 90; Total fat: 9g; Saturated fat: 5g; Total carbs: 1g; Fiber: 0g; Cholesterol: 73mg; Protein: 1g

Cranberry Sauce

Makes about 2 cups • Serving size = about 2 tablespoons

Cranberry sauce is a classic recipe that is traditionally served at Thanksgiving. It can, however, be enjoyed all year-round as a complement to steamed vegetables or even served over steamed rice.

4 cups fresh cranberries

1 cup water

1 cup granulated sugar

1 tablespoon orange zest

1 cup raisins

1. Rinse the cranberries well and set them aside.

2. Bring the water and sugar to boil in a medium saucepan, stirring until the sugar is fully dissolved.

3. Add the cranberries and bring to a boil.

4. Reduce the heat and simmer for 10 to 12 minutes until the cranberries burst.

5. Stir in the orange zest and raisins; remove from heat.

6. Cool to room temperature; chill in the refrigerator before serving.

Per Serving Calories 64; Total fat: 0g; Saturated fat: 0g; Total carbs: 17g; Fiber: 1g; Cholesterol: 0mg; Protein: 0g

Roasted Garlic Sauce

Makes about 1 cup • Serving size = about 2 tablespoons

This roasted garlic sauce is full of flavor, ideal for drizzling over steamed veggies or tossing with braised greens.

3 whole garlic cloves

1½ teaspoons olive oil

1 teaspoon white wine

¾ cup heavy cream

3 to 4 tablespoons grated Parmesan cheese

Salt and pepper

1. Preheat oven to 400°F.

2. Cut a small square of aluminum foil and place the garlic cloves in the center.

3. Drizzle with olive oil and then fold the foil into a pouch.

4. Roast the garlic in the oven for 30 minutes and then set aside until cool enough to handle.

5. Squeeze the garlic cloves out of the skin into a bowl and mash with the back of a spoon.

6. Transfer the garlic to a small saucepan and stir in the white wine.

7. Whisk in the heavy cream and reduce the heat until the sauce begins to thicken.

8. Stir in the Parmesan cheese, whisking until the mixture is smooth.

9. Remove from heat and season with salt and pepper.

Per Serving Calories 100; Total fat: 10g; Saturated fat: 6g; Total carbs: 2g; Fiber: 0g; Cholesterol: 33mg; Protein: 2g

Marinara Sauce

Makes about 4 cups • Serving size = about ¼ cup

Homemade marinara sauce is nothing like what you buy in the grocery store. It has a deep, bold flavor and is simply divine when poured over fresh pasta.

½ cup olive oil

1 tablespoon chopped garlic

1 medium onion, diced

2 celery stalks, diced

2 medium carrots, diced

1 poblano pepper, seeded and diced

½ teaspoon salt

½ teaspoon fresh ground pepper

Two 28-ounce cans crushed tomatoes

2 bay leaves

¼ cup red wine

1. Heat the oil in a stockpot over medium-high heat.

2. Add the garlic and cook for 1 minute.

3. Stir in the onion and cook for 8 to 10 minutes until translucent.

4. Add the celery, carrots, poblano pepper, salt, and pepper.

5. Cook for 8 to 10 minutes until all the vegetables are tender.

6. Stir in the tomatoes, bay leaves, and red wine.

7. Reduce the heat and simmer the sauce, uncovered, for 1 hour.

8. Remove the bay leaves and remove from heat.

9. Allow to cool slightly until ready to use.

Per Serving Calories 84; Total fat: 6g; Saturated fat: 1g; Total carbs: 6g; Fiber: 2g; Cholesterol: 0mg; Protein: 1g

Peanut Sauce

Serves 4 • Serving size = about 2 tablespoons

This sauce is warm and creamy, full of peanut flavor with just a hint of soy and honey. Toss this sauce into hot noodles or drizzle it over a crisp salad.

¼ cup smooth peanut butter

¼ cup water

¼ cup low-sodium soy sauce

1 tablespoon fresh lemon juice

1½ tablespoons raw honey

½ cup orange juice

Pinch ground ginger

1. Combine the peanut butter, water, and soy sauce in a small saucepan over low heat.

2. Whisk in the remaining ingredients and stir until the sauce is smooth and melted.

3. Remove from heat and cool slightly before using.

Per Serving Calories 139; Total fat: 8g; Saturated fat: 2g; Total carbs: 14g; Fiber: 1g; Cholesterol: 0mg; Protein: 5g

Basil Pine Nut Pesto

Makes about 1½ cups • Serving size = about 2 tablespoons

Pesto is a great spread for sandwiches, and it can also be used as a dip for fresh cut veggies. In this recipe, the flavor of fresh pine nuts is perfectly balanced with the taste of fresh basil and a hint of lemon juice.

4 cups fresh basil leaves, packed

1 cup freshly grated Parmesan cheese

½ cup toasted pine nuts

5 garlic cloves, peeled

1 cup olive oil

Salt and pepper

1. Place the basil leaves in a food processor and add the Parmesan cheese, pine nuts, and garlic.

2. Pulse to finely chop and then blend to purée.

3. With the food processor running, drizzle in the olive oil.

4. Season with salt and pepper; let stand for 5 minutes before using.

Per Serving Calories 216; Total fat: 23g; Saturated fat: 4g; Total carbs: 2g; Fiber: 0g; Cholesterol: 7mg; Protein: 4g

Sweet Corn and Red Pepper Relish

Makes about 8 cups • Serving size = about 2 tablespoons

This sweet corn and red pepper relish works well in quesadillas, on top of steamed veggies, or as a dip for tortilla chips. Get creative—you never know what delicious combinations are just waiting to be discovered!

3 pounds heirloom tomatoes

3 cups corn kernels cut from the cob

2 medium red peppers, diced

1½ cups cider vinegar

1 small red onion, diced

⅔ cup granulated sugar

¼ cup fresh lime juice

1½ teaspoons ground cumin

1 teaspoon coarse salt

½ teaspoon red pepper flakes

1. Prepare four 1-pint canning jars by boiling them in a large pot of water for 10 minutes.

2. Leave the jars in the water until you are ready to fill them.

3. Bring another pot of water to a boil.

4. Use a sharp knife to score an X in the bottom of each tomato and blanch them in the hot water for 1 to 2 minutes.

5. Immediately transfer the tomatoes to a bowl of ice water and then peel off the skins.

6. Chop the tomatoes, reserving the juice on the cutting board.

7. Transfer the chopped tomato and the reserved juice to a saucepan and stir in the remaining ingredients.

8. Bring to a boil and then reduce heat and simmer for 20 minutes until the liquid has cooked off.

9. Spoon the relish into the jars, leaving about ½ inch of space at the top of each jar.

10. Seal the jars and place them back into the boiling water for 15 minutes.

11. Cool the jars at room temperature and store in the refrigerator.

Per Serving Calories 21; Total fat: 0g; Saturated fat: 0g; Total carbs: 5g; Fiber: 1g; Cholesterol: 0mg; Protein: 1g

ELEVEN

Fruit-Focused

The recipes in this chapter were designed with fruitarians in mind. While not all of the recipes conform to the strict guidelines of the fruitarian diet, fruit and nuts play the starring role. In this chapter you will find quick and easy recipes like smoothies and fruit pops, as well as unique recipes such as Easy Fruit Sushi and Buckwheat Pancakes with Kiwi.

RECILPES

Easy Date Butter

This creamy date butter is a great dip for celery sticks—spread it thick on celery sticks and top with raisins or crushed walnuts.

1 cup pitted dates
⅓ cup boiling water

1. Place the dates in a food processor and blend into a paste, adding the water 1 tablespoon at a time.

2. Blend until smooth and store in the refrigerator.

Per Serving Calories 63; Total fat: 0g; Saturated fat: 0g; Total carbs: 17g; Fiber: 2g; Cholesterol: 0mg; Protein: 1g

Strawberry Rhubarb Preserves

Makes about 6 pints • Serving size = 2 tablespoons

While many vegetables lose some of their health benefits in the cooking process, rhubarb is the opposite. This vegetable contains polyphenols, which help to prevent cancer, and they are "activated" by exposure to heat.

4 cups fresh strawberries, chopped

2 cups chopped rhubarb

4 tablespoons fresh lemon juice

1 envelope powdered fruit pectin

5½ cups granulated sugar

1. Mash the strawberries with a fork and transfer them to a saucepan.

2. Stir in the rhubarb, lemon juice, and pectin; bring to a boil.

3. Stir in the sugar and bring to a boil; cook for 1 minute.

4. Remove from heat and skim off the foam.

5. Spoon the mixture into pint jars, leaving a ¼- to ½-inch space at the top of the jar.

6. Process the jars in boiling water for about 5 minutes.

Per Serving Calories 65; Total fat: 0g; Saturated fat: 0g; Total carbs: 17g; Fiber: 0g; Cholesterol: 0mg; Protein: 0g

Blueberry Jam

Makes about 4 pints • Serving size = about 2 tablespoons

This blueberry jam is the perfect topping for crisp toast, and it always works well spread on hot pancakes or waffles.

4 pints fresh blueberries

6 cups granulated sugar

2 tablespoons fresh lemon juice

1 tablespoon lemon zest

1 teaspoon ground cinnamon

6 ounces liquid fruit pectin

1. Place the blueberries in a food processor and blend until smooth.

2. Pour the blueberry purée into a medium saucepan and whisk in the sugar, lemon juice, lemon zest, and cinnamon.

3. Bring the mixture to a boil and stir in the fruit pectin.

4. Boil the mixture for 1 minute while stirring; remove from heat.

5. Skim off the foam and ladle into half-pint jars, leaving about a ¼- to ½-inch space at the top.

6. Top with a lid and process in boiling water for 10 minutes.

Per Serving Calories 86; Total fat: 0g; Saturated fat: 0g; Total carbs: 23g; Fiber: 1g; Cholesterol: 0mg; Protein: 0g

Berry Blast Juice

Makes 2 servings

This berry blast juice combines the nutritional power of beets with the sweetness of mixed berries. This juice is a great option for breakfast, but it also makes a delicious snack.

1 cup fresh mixed berries

2 medium beets

2 large celery stalks

½ bunch fresh cilantro leaves

1. Rinse all of the ingredients in fresh water.

2. Trim or cut the ingredients as needed to fit into the juicer.

3. Place a container under the juicer's spout.

4. Feed the ingredients one at a time, in the order listed, through the juicer.

5. Stir the resulting juice and pour into glasses to serve.

Per Serving Calories 55; Total fat: 0g; Saturated fat: 0g; Total carbs: 16g; Fiber: 1g; Cholesterol: 0mg; Protein: 3g

Mango Peach Smoothie

Serves 2

Mango is an excellent source of vitamin A and vitamin C, both of which help to strengthen the immune system. This smoothie is full of nutrients as well as fresh fruit flavor.

2 cups frozen
mango chunks

1 cup organic orange juice

1 ripe peach, pitted
and chopped

½ cup plain nonfat yogurt

1. Combine the mango and orange juice in a blender and blend until smooth.

2. Add the remaining ingredients and blend on high speed for 20 to 30 seconds until smooth and well combined.

3. Pour into two glasses and serve immediately.

Per Serving Calories 219; Total fat: 1g; Saturated fat: 1g; Total carbs: 48g; Fiber: 4g; Cholesterol: 4mg; Protein: 5g

Strawberry Apple Kale Smoothie

Serves 2

This strawberry apple kale smoothie is packed with flavor and nutrients—it is a great snack to tide you over between meals, or it can act as a meal in and of itself!

2 large leaves kale, chopped

1 cup orange juice

1 cup frozen strawberries

1 medium apple, cored and chopped

½ cup plain nonfat yogurt

1. Combine the kale leaves and orange juice in a blender and blend until smooth.

2. Add the remaining ingredients and blend on high speed for 20 to 30 seconds until smooth and well combined.

3. Pour into two glasses and serve immediately.

Per Serving Calories 199; Total fat: 1g; Saturated fat: 1g; Total carbs: 43g; Fiber: 5g; Cholesterol: 4mg; Protein: 6g

Blueberry Banana Coconut Smoothie

Blueberries are rich in flavonoids and a dietary fiber called pectin, both of which may help to reduce the risk for type 2 diabetes. These berries are also full of vitamin C, manganese, and potassium.

2 cups frozen blueberries

1 cup unsweetened coconut milk

2 frozen bananas, chopped

1 tablespoon raw honey

1. Combine the blueberries and coconut milk in a blender and blend until smooth.

2. Add the remaining ingredients and blend on high speed for 20 to 30 seconds until smooth and well combined.

3. Pour into two glasses and serve immediately.

Per Serving Calories 258; Total fat: 3g; Saturated fat: 2g; Total carbs: 62g; Fiber: 8g; Cholesterol: 0mg; Protein: 3g

Frozen Banana Pudding

Serves 3 to 4 • Serving size = about ½ cup

Bananas are packed full of B vitamins, which is essential for promoting healthy sleep and also helps reduce irritability and mood swings. After tasting this delicious frozen pudding, you will find it hard to be anything but positively cheerful.

4 frozen bananas, halved

Pinch of ground cinnamon

1. Place a bowl under the spout of an electric juicer.

2. Feed the frozen banana halves through the juicer and collect the pudding in the bowl.

3. Divide among dessert cups and sprinkle with cinnamon to serve.

Per Serving Calories 162; Total fat: 1g; Saturated fat: 0g; Total carbs: 42g; Fiber: 5g; Cholesterol: 0mg; Protein: 2g

Fruit Smoothie Pops

These fruit pops have all the flavor of your favorite fruit smoothie in a cool, frozen treat. Don't be afraid to try different flavor combinations with whatever fruit you have on hand.

1 ripe banana, peeled and chopped

1 cup sliced strawberries

2 cups pineapple juice

1 cup apple juice

1 cup orange juice

1. Combine all of the ingredients in a blender and blend until smooth.

2. Pour the mixture into 12 ice pop molds and freeze until solid.

Per Serving Calories 55; Total fat: 0g; Saturated fat: 0g; Total carbs: 14g; Fiber: 1g; Cholesterol: 0mg; Protein: 1g

Easy Fruit Sushi

Serves 2 to 3

If you are looking for a quick and easy snack, this fruit sushi is a great option. Try using different kinds of fruit to switch up the flavors.

1 large cucumber

1 medium apple, cored

½ cup fresh strawberries, chopped

½ avocado, pitted and chopped

1. Slice the cucumber into thin strips, lengthwise.

2. Cut the apple and strawberries into matchsticks.

3. Place several apple, avocado, and strawberry pieces in the middle of each cucumber strip.

4. Roll the cucumber up around the fruit and secure with a toothpick.

5. Chill until ready to serve.

Per Serving Calories 195; Total fat: 10g; Saturated fat: 2g; Total carbs: 28g; Fiber: 8g; Cholesterol: 0mg; Protein: 3g

Tropical Melon Fruit Cup

Serves 4 to 5 • Serving size = About 1 cup

This tropical melon fruit cup is the perfect blend of tropical fruits—melon, mango, banana, and pineapple flavored with a hint of lemon juice and fresh mint.

1 ripe honeydew melon

1 mango, pitted and chopped

1 banana, peeled and chopped

1 ripe pineapple, cored and husked

1 tablespoon fresh lemon juice

1 tablespoon fresh chopped mint

1. Cut the honeydew in half using a sharp knife.

2. Scoop out and discard the seeds; then peel the melon and chop the flesh.

3. Transfer the melon to a bowl and add the mango and banana.

4. Chop the pineapple and add it to the bowl; stir to combine.

5. Stir in the lemon juice and chopped mint and toss to coat.

6. Chill the fruit until ready to serve.

Per Serving Calories 234; Total fat: 1g; Saturated fat: 0g; Total carbs: 59g; Fiber: 6g; Cholesterol: 0mg; Protein: 3g

Fruitarian Breakfast Cup

Serves 1

This breakfast cup is simple to prepare but full of flavor. Try mixing it up with different berries or substitute another type of dried fruit for the raisins.

1 large banana, peeled and sliced

½ cup apple juice

1 teaspoon raw honey

2 tablespoons chopped walnuts

2 tablespoons raisins

1 cup fresh raspberries

1. Place the banana in a bowl and mash with a fork.

2. Stir in the apple juice, honey, walnuts, and raisins.

3. Sprinkle with raspberries and serve.

Per Serving Calories 365; Total fat: 3g; Saturated fat: 0g; Total carbs: 88g; Fiber: 13g; Cholesterol: 0mg; Protein: 4g

Sesame Mango Avocado Salad

Serves 4 to 6 • Serving size = about ½ cup

This mango avocado salad is sweet and refreshing, full of fresh fruit flavor. The sweetness of the mango is perfectly paired with ripe avocado and tied together with fresh cilantro.

2 ripe mangos, pitted and chopped

1 ripe avocado, pitted and chopped

2 tablespoons chopped cilantro leaves

1 navel orange, juiced

1 lime, juiced

2 teaspoons olive oil

1 tablespoon toasted sesame seeds

1. Combine the mangos, avocado, and cilantro in a bowl and stir well.

2. For the dressing: Whisk together the remaining ingredients and pour over the salad.

3. Toss to coat.

4. Chill until ready to serve.

Per Serving Calories 248; Total fat: 14g; Saturated fat: 3g; Total carbs: 33g; Fiber: 6g; Cholesterol: 0mg; Protein: 3g

Buckwheat Pancakes with Kiwi

Serves 5 to 6 • Serving size = 2 pancakes with ¼ cup fruit purée

Despite the name, buckwheat flour is completely wheat- and gluten-free. These buckwheat pancakes are a great option for individuals with gluten intolerance.

½ cup old-fashioned oats

½ cup raw cashews

1 cup buckwheat flour

½ cup water

1 cup fresh raspberries

2 ripe kiwis, peeled and sliced

Canola oil

Raw honey

1. Combine the oats and cashews in a food processor and blend until finely powdered.

2. Transfer the mixture to a bowl and whisk in the buckwheat flour.

3. Whisk in water to create a smooth batter; add more water if necessary.

4. Combine the raspberries and kiwis in a blender and purée until smooth.

5. Heat a nonstick skillet over medium heat.

6. Add 1 teaspoon canola oil and spoon ¼ cup batter into the skillet.

7. Cook the pancake until bubbles form on the surface; then flip the pancake and cook until lightly browned on the underside.

8. Transfer the pancake to a plate and repeat with the remaining batter.

9. Serve the pancakes with the fruit purée spooned over them, drizzled with honey.

Per Serving Calories 220; Total fat: 8g; Saturated fat: 1g; Total carbs: 35g; Fiber: 6g; Cholesterol: 0mg; Protein: 5g

Berries and Cream Crêpes

Makes about 12 crêpes • Serving size = about 2 crêpes

These berries and cream crêpes are the perfect blend of sweet fruit flavor and cream cheese. Enjoy these crêpes at breakfast or use them as a dessert.

2 cups fresh raspberries

2 cups fresh strawberries

1 cup light brown sugar, packed

1 teaspoon vanilla extract

8 ounces light cream cheese, at room temperature

½ cup powdered sugar

1 teaspoon fresh lemon juice

¾ cup plus 2 tablespoons all-purpose flour

¼ cup granulated sugar

1¼ cups whole milk

3 eggs, beaten

1. Place the berries in a food processor and blend to purée.

2. Pour the mixture into a saucepan and bring to a simmer.

3. Whisk in the brown sugar and vanilla extract and remove from heat.

4. Beat the cream cheese and powdered sugar in a bowl with the lemon juice until smooth.

5. Whisk together the flour and sugar in a mixing bowl.

6. In a separate bowl, whisk together the milk and eggs.

7. Pour the egg mixture into the flour mixture while whisking until the batter is smooth.

8. Heat a skillet over medium heat and spray with cooking spray.

9. Spoon about ¼ cup of batter into the skillet and swirl to coat.

→

10. Cook the batter until the crêpe is lightly browned; then flip it and cook for 1 minute more.

11. Transfer the crêpe to a plate and repeat with the remaining batter.

12. Spoon the cream cheese mixture down the center of each crêpe and roll the crêpe up around the filling.

13. Drizzle with the berry mixture to serve.

Per Serving Calories 557; Total fat: 20g; Saturated fat: 12g; Total carbs: 84g; Fiber: 4g; Cholesterol: 135mg; Protein: 15g

Fresh Fruit Tart

Serves 6 to 8

This fresh fruit tart is beautiful to behold. Colorful and full of fresh fruit flavor, it is a dessert that is almost too pretty to eat.

¼ cup plus 1 tablespoon vegan shortening

⅓ cup all-purpose flour

Pinch of salt

3 to 4 tablespoons ice water

6 tablespoons vegan butter spread

1 cup tofu cream cheese

3½ to 4 cups powdered sugar

1 teaspoon almond extract

1 ripe peach, pitted and thinly sliced

1 ripe kiwi, peeled and thinly sliced

½ cup fresh strawberries, sliced

½ cup fresh blackberries

¼ cup fresh blueberries maple syrup (optional)

1. Preheat oven to 375°F.

2. Place the shortening in a mixing bowl and beat by hand until smooth.

3. Beat in the flour and salt until well combined.

4. Add the ice water 1 tablespoon at a time, beating for 10 to 15 seconds after each addition.

5. Beat the mixture until it forms a dough but do not overbeat.

6. Turn the dough out onto a floured surface and roll it out into a ¼-inch-thick circle.

7. Carefully transfer the dough to a parchment-lined baking sheet and bake for 10 to 15 minutes until lightly browned.

8. Beat together the vegan butter spread and tofu cream cheese in a mixing bowl.

9. Add the powdered sugar in small batches, beating until smooth.

10. Taste the mixture after 3 cups of sugar have been added and add more, if desired, up to 1 cup.

11. Beat in the almond extract and then spread evenly on the crust.

12. Arrange the sliced fruit and berries on top of the crust and chill; drizzle with maple syrup to serve, if desired.

Per Serving Calories 569; Total fat: 23g; Saturated fat: 7g; Total carbs: 92g; Fiber: 2g; Cholesterol: 0mg; Protein: 4g

TWELVE

Raw Food

Eating raw food is a great way to get all the natural enzymes from food as well as vitamins and minerals in their natural combinations. Proponents of raw food diets believe that the best way to get the maximum health benefits of fresh food is to eat it raw. Most raw food diets consist of 75 percent fruits and vegetables, supplemented with seeds, sprouts, beans, nuts, and dried fruit. Rather than using a traditional oven to prepare foods, followers of raw food diets use an appliance called a dehydrator to slow cook foods to a temperature no greater than 115°F.

RECIPES

Raw Cashew Cream

Makes about 1 cup • Serving size = about 2 tablespoons

This cashew cream is a staple ingredient in many raw food recipes. Use it as a dip for fresh fruit and vegetables or stir it into your favorite pudding.

1 cup cashews

1 cup water

1 ripe pear, cored and chopped

1 tablespoon raw honey

1. Place the cashews in a food processor and blend into a fine powder.

2. Add the water and blend again until smooth.

3. Blend in the pear and honey until smooth.

Per Serving Calories 50; Total fat: 2g; Saturated fat: 0g; Total carbs: 7g; Fiber: 1g; Cholesterol: 0mg; Protein: 1g

Raw Apple Cream

Serves 4 • Serving size = about ½ cup

This raw apple cream is a great recipe to have on hand for a tasty snack or dessert. Enjoy it on its own or use it as a dip or topping for fresh fruit.

¾ cup raisins

Water

4 ripe apples, cored and chopped

1. Place the raisins in a bowl and cover with water.

2. Let the raisins soak for 2 to 4 hours and then drain, reserving about ½ cup of the liquid.

3. Combine the water, raisins, and apples in a food processor and blend until creamy.

4. Serve the cream as a dessert or with fruit.

Per Serving Calories 157; Total fat: 0g; Saturated fat: 0g; Total carbs: 42g; Fiber: 6g; Cholesterol: 0mg; Protein: 1g

Raw Chocolate Milk

Surprisingly, milk is not actually on the list of ingredients for this recipe. By using a combination of cashew cream, water, and cocoa, with a little honey for sweetness, you can make a delicious raw chocolate beverage.

1 cup cashew cream

⅓ cup water

2 tablespoons unsweetened cocoa

1 tablespoon raw honey

1. Combine the cashew cream and water in a blender and blend until smooth.

2. Add the remaining ingredients and blend until well combined.

3. Pour into two glasses and serve immediately.

Per Serving Calories 308; Total fat: 13g; Saturated fat: 12g; Total carbs: 51g; Fiber: 2g; Cholesterol: 0mg; Protein: 2g

Raw Chai Smoothie

If you are looking for a refreshing raw beverage, look no further than this chai smoothie. Made with raw flaxseed and sweetened with pitted dates, this is sure to satisfy your sweet tooth as well as your thirst.

1 cup raw flaxseed

2 cups water

5 pitted dates

1 tablespoon honey

1 teaspoon cinnamon powder

Pinch ground cloves

1. Place the flaxseed and water in a blender and blend until smooth.

2. Add the remaining ingredients and blend until well combined.

3. Pour into two glasses and serve immediately.

Per Serving Calories 574; Total fat: 28g; Saturated fat: 0g; Total carbs: 65g; Fiber: 34g; Cholesterol: 0mg; Protein: 25g

Raw Stuffed Apples

Serves 4

Everybody loves stuffed apples and these raw stuffed apples are sure to please. Bursting with an almond, honey, and cinnamon mixture, these apples are truly delectable.

4 ripe apples

1 cup raw almonds

1 tablespoon raw honey

2 teaspoons ground cinnamon

1. Core the apples and scoop out about two-thirds of the pulp using a melon baller.

2. Place the almonds in a food processor and blend into a fine flour.

3. Add the apple pulp, honey, and cinnamon and blend until well combined.

4. Spoon the mixture into the cored apples and serve immediately.

Per Serving Calories 272; Total fat: 12g; Saturated fat: 1g; Total carbs: 41g; Fiber: 9g; Cholesterol: 0mg; Protein: 6g

Raw Power Squares

These power squares are great for snacks or dessert. They have plenty of monounsaturated (heart-healthy) fat along with protein and other vital nutrients.

1¾ cups chopped walnuts, divided

2 tablespoons pure maple syrup

1 tablespoon water

2 tablespoons coconut oil

½ cup unsweetened shredded coconut

2 tablespoons unsweetened cocoa powder

½ teaspoon vanilla extract

Pinch ground nutmeg

1. Finely chop ¼ cup walnuts and set aside.

2. Place the remaining walnuts in a food processor and blend until it forms a coarse flour.

3. Transfer the flour to a bowl and stir in the remaining ingredients.

4. Stir until the mixture is thick and well combined.

5. Pat the mixture into a dish to 1-inch thickness.

6. Cover and chill until firm (about 1 hour) and cut into 1-inch squares.

Per Serving Calories 222; Total fat: 20g; Saturated fat: 7g; Total carbs: 9g; Fiber: 3g; Cholesterol: 0mg; Protein: 4g

Raw Banana Walnut Pancakes

Serves 2 • Serving size = 3 Pancakes

If you like to have some quick breakfast options around in the morning, make up a batch or two of these raw pancakes over the weekend. By cooking them in your dehydrator overnight, you can wake up to a freshly prepared meal.

1½ cups ground flaxseed

½ cup whole flaxseed

½ cup unsweetened coconut, dried

¾ cup water

¼ cup raw honey

¼ cup coconut butter

1 cup banana, sliced

¾ cup chopped walnuts

1. Combine all of the ingredients in a bowl and mix well.

2. Spoon the mixture onto the trays of your dehydrator and cook for 1 hour at 140°F.

3. Flip the pancakes; then lower the heat and dehydrate at 114°F for 30 minutes.

Per Serving Calories 1386; Total fat: 106g; Saturated fat: 36g; Total carbs: 101g; Fiber: 42g; Cholesterol: 0mg; Protein: 30g

Raw Blueberry Flaxseed Pancakes

Makes 5 to 6 pancakes • Serving size = 3 small pancakes

Flaxseed is a good source of vegetarian protein as well as dietary fiber. Combined with the nutritional power of fresh blueberries, these raw pancakes are a great way to start your day!

½ cup ground flaxseed

1 cup whole flaxseed

3 tablespoons coconut oil, melted

¼ cup raw honey

½ cup water

1 cup fresh blueberries

¼ cup unsweetened dried coconut

1. Combine all of the ingredients in a bowl and mix well.

2. Spoon the mixture onto the trays of your dehydrator and cook for 1 hour at 145°F.

3. Flip the pancakes and then lower the heat and dehydrate at 114°F for 30 minutes.

Per Serving Calories 999; Total fat: 74g; Saturated fat: 29g; Total carbs: 79g; Fiber: 33g; Cholesterol: 0mg; Protein: 21g

Raw Stuffed Mushrooms

Makes 2 cups • Serving size = about 4 mushrooms

These raw stuffed mushrooms are a great appetizer to have around for dinner parties or family get-togethers. Even guests who do not follow a raw food diet are sure to love them.

4 cups whole mushrooms, divided

¼ cup olive oil

¼ cup raw soy sauce (nama shoyu)

1 tablespoon raw honey

1 teaspoon minced garlic

1 cup soaked pumpkin seeds

1 cup soaked sunflower seeds

¼ cup fresh chopped parsley

Salt and pepper

1. Set aside 2 cups of mushrooms and remove the stems from the remaining 2 cups.

2. Whisk together the olive oil, soy sauce, and honey in a bowl.

3. Add the stemmed mushrooms and toss to coat.

4. Let sit for 3 hours, stirring occasionally.

5. Place the garlic in a food processor along with the remaining 2 cups of mushrooms.

6. Blend until finely chopped and then transfer to a bowl.

7. Combine the pumpkin seeds and sunflower seeds in the food processor and blend into a paste.

8. Stir the seed paste into the garlic and mushroom mixture; then stir in the parsley, salt, and pepper.

9. Spoon the filling into the stemmed mushrooms and serve immediately.

Per Serving Calories 258; Total fat: 22g; Saturated fat: 3g; Total carbs: 10g; Fiber: 3g; Cholesterol: 0mg; Protein: 9g

Raw Mushroom Burgers

Serves 4 to 6 • Serving size = 1 burger

Your dehydrator can be used for more than just making fruit or vegetable chips. You can also use it to make these delicious raw mushroom burgers!

2 cups chopped portobello mushrooms

2 cups grated carrots

1 cup diced red onion

½ cup diced celery

1 cup soaked walnuts, finely ground

½ cup ground pumpkin seeds

4 tablespoons water

4 tablespoons raw soy sauce (nama shoyu)

1 teaspoon dried thyme

1 cup oat flour

1. Stir together the mushrooms, carrots, onion, and celery.

2. Stir in the ground walnuts and pumpkin seeds.

3. Whisk together the water and raw soy sauce and then stir into the vegetable mixture.

4. Stir in the thyme and oat flour; then shape the mixture into patties between ½- and 1-inch thick.

5. Arrange the patties on the screens of your dehydrator and cook for 1 hour at 140°F.

6. Reduce the heat and cook for 3 to 4 hours at 115°F.

Per Serving Calories 286; Total fat: 15g; Saturated fat: 2g; Total carbs: 30g; Fiber: 6g; Cholesterol: 0mg; Protein: 11g

Raw Cilantro Avocado Veggie Wraps

Serves 1

If you are looking for a quick and filling meal, these raw cilantro avocado veggie wraps are just the thing. Made with lettuce wraps instead of tortillas and stuffed with fresh vegetables, these wraps are a raw foodist's dream.

2 leaves Boston lettuce

½ ripe avocado, pitted and sliced

1 small carrot, grated

1 scallion, chopped

¼ cup cucumber, thinly sliced

2 tablespoons thinly sliced red onion

¼ cup fresh chopped cilantro leaves

1 tablespoon fresh lemon juice

1 tablespoon fresh lime juice

1 teaspoon raw honey

1. Lay the lettuce leaves out flat on a plate to form a cup.

2. Divide the avocado, carrot, scallion, cucumber, and red onion evenly between the two lettuce cups.

3. Top each with about 2 tablespoons fresh cilantro.

4. Whisk together the remaining ingredients and drizzle over the vegetables.

5. Wrap the lettuce up around the filling and serve immediately.

Per Serving Calories 252; Total fat: 20g; Saturated fat: 4g; Total carbs: 19g; Fiber: 8g; Cholesterol: 0mg; Protein: 3g

Raw Spinach Quiche

Serves 2 to 3

Spinach is an excellent source of vegetarian protein, which is why it is an excellent substitute for eggs in this vegetarian raw quiche.

1 medium carrot, diced

½ shallot

1 cup toasted pine nuts

½ cup pumpkin seeds

1 cup soaked cashews

½ cup fresh lemon juice

¼ cup olive oil

1 garlic clove, minced

2 cups baby spinach

½ cup sun-dried tomatoes, chopped

1 cup cherry, tomatoes halved

1. Combine the first four ingredients in a food processor and blend until it begins to stick together.

2. Press the mixture into a small pie plate and dehydrate for 30 minutes at 145°F (you can also dehydrate it for 6 hours at 114°F).

3. Place the cashews in a food processor and add the lemon juice and olive oil.

4. Blend until smooth; add the garlic.

5. Process until smooth and then blend in 1 cup of baby spinach.

6. Spoon the mixture into a bowl and chop the remaining 1 cup spinach by hand before stirring it in along with the sun-dried tomatoes.

7. Scoop about ¾ cup of this mixture into the quiche crust and save the rest as a spread for crackers.

8. Top the quiche with cherry tomato halves to serve.

9. Chill for several hours before serving.

Per Serving Calories 1275; Total fat: 113g; Saturated fat: 15g; Total carbs: 48g; Fiber: 10g; Cholesterol: 0mg; Protein: 32g

Raw Chocolate-Covered Pecans

Makes 1 cup • Serving size = about 2 tablespoons

These chocolate-covered pecans are coated with homemade chocolate sauce and chilled to perfection. Keep a few stashed in your refrigerator for those days when you just need a bite of chocolate to pick you up.

1 cup coconut oil

⅔ cup unsweetened cocoa powder

¼ cup raw honey

½ cup chopped walnuts

1 cup pecan halves

1. Melt the coconut oil in a small saucepan and then stir in the cocoa powder, honey, and walnuts.

2. Whisk until smooth and set aside.

3. Dip the pecans in the chocolate sauce and arrange on a parchment-lined tray.

4. Refrigerate until ready to serve.

Per Serving Calories 321; Total fat: 32g; Saturated fat: 24g; Total carbs: 13g; Fiber: 3g; Cholesterol: 0mg; Protein: 2g

Raw Chocolate Truffles

Makes 10 truffles • Serving size = 1 truffle

No one ever said that raw food can't be delicious—these raw chocolate truffles are as good (or better) than any traditional candies you've ever had.

½ cup cacao butter

¼ cup coconut oil

6 tablespoons unsweetened cocoa powder

3 tablespoons raw honey

1. Cut the cacao butter into cubes and melt them in a double boiler over hot water.

2. Stir in the coconut oil, cocoa powder, and raw honey until well blended.

3. Pour the mixture into an ice cube tray and refrigerate until firm, about 2 hours.

Per Serving Calories 173; Total fat: 17g; Saturated fat: 12g; Total carbs: 7g; Fiber: 1g; Cholesterol: 0mg; Protein: 1g

Raw Raspberry "Ice Cream"

Despite the name, this recipe does not include any actual cream; in fact, it is completely dairy-free. Made with two simple ingredients, this treat is definitely something to scream over.

1 frozen bananas, sliced

1 cup frozen raspberries

1. Let the frozen fruit sit at room temperature for about 5 minutes.

2. Place the bananas and raspberries in a blender and process until smooth.

3. Spoon into two ice cream dishes to serve.

Per Serving Calories 189; Total fat: 0g; Saturated fat: 0g; Total carbs: 48g; Fiber: 7g; Cholesterol: 0mg; Protein: 2g

Raw Cinnamon Cookies

Makes about 2 dozen cookies • Serving size = 1 cookie

These raw cinnamon cookies are bursting with cinnamon and raisin flavor. They are sure to become a family favorite!

2 cups old-fashioned oats

⅔ cup pitted medjool dates

½ cup raisins

½ cup chopped cashews

½ to 1 cup unsweetened applesauce

1. Place the oats in a food processor and blend until ground into a fine flour.

2. Add the dates and blend until it forms a sticky batter.

3. Transfer the batter to a mixing bowl and stir in the raisins and cashews.

4. Using your hands to mix, blend in ¼ cup applesauce at a time until the batter is pliable but holds together.

5. Shape the batter into cookies and arrange them on the trays of your dehydrator.

6. Cook at 108°F for 8 to 12 hours.

Per Serving Calories 56; Total fat: 2g; Saturated fat: 0g; Total carbs: 10g; Fiber: 1g; Cholesterol: 0mg; Protein: 1g

Raw Chocolate Chip Cookies

Makes about 2 dozen • Serving size = 1 cookie

These chocolate chip cookies are guaranteed to satisfy your sweet tooth and, because they are made with only three ingredients, you don't have to worry about them being bad for you!

1 cup raw cashews

2½ tablespoons raw honey

⅓ cup cacao nibs

1. Place the cashews in a food processor and blend into a fine flour.

2. Add the honey and blend well; transfer to a bowl.

3. Stir in the cacao nibs and shape the mixture into cookies.

4. Arrange the cookies on the trays of a dehydrator and bake for 8 to 12 hours at 108°F, rotating the pans after 4 to 6 hours.

Per Serving Calories 26; Total fat: 1g; Saturated fat: 1g; Total carbs: 3g; Fiber: 1g; Cholesterol: 0mg; Protein: 1g

Raw Mixed Berry Pie

Serves 6

Berries are an excellent source of vitamin C and, in this recipe, their nutritional value is not compromised by cooking. This pie is fresh and delicious, relying only on the natural flavor of ripe berries.

2½ cups chopped walnuts

7 apricots

1⅓ cups shredded coconut, unsweetened

½ cup fresh lime juice

1 tablespoon raw honey

1 ripe kiwi, peeled and sliced

2 cups sliced strawberries

½ cup fresh blueberries

½ cup fresh raspberries

1. In separate bowls, cover the walnuts and apricots with water and soak for up to 24 hours.

2. Combine the soaked walnuts, soaked apricots, and shredded coconut in a food processor and blend until smooth.

3. Add the lime juice, honey, and kiwi, and blend until well combined. Add some water from the apricot soak, if needed.

4. Press the mixture into the bottom of a pie plate and top with fresh berries.

Per Serving Calories 233; Total fat: 16g; Saturated fat: 7g; Total carbs: 22g; Fiber: 5g; Cholesterol: 0mg; Protein: 4g

Raw Banana Mint Pie

Serves 6

Banana and mint may sound like a strange combination of flavors, but in this recipe they combine deliciously in a smooth, ice cream-like filling.

6 frozen bananas, peeled and sliced

2 cups raw almonds

1 cup shredded unsweetened coconut, divided

10 pitted medjool dates

Pinch of salt

1 teaspoon vanilla extract

4 drops peppermint oil

1. Defrost the bananas at room temperature for 10 to 15 minutes.

2. Place the almonds in a food processor and blend into a fine flour.

3. Add ½ cup of coconut along with the dates and salt; blend until it begins to stick together.

4. Press the mixture into the bottom of a pie plate.

5. Combine the bananas, remaining ½ cup of coconut, vanilla extract, and peppermint oil in a food processor until smooth.

6. Spoon the filling into the crust and serve immediately.

Per Serving Calories 577; Total fat: 30g; Saturated fat: 7g; Total carbs: 74g; Fiber: 14g; Cholesterol: 0mg; Protein: 14g

Raw Strawberry Banana Cake

This raw strawberry banana cake is the perfect dessert to bring along to a family picnic or get-together. You don't even need to tell everyone the cake is raw—they are sure to love it!

1 cup cashews

1 cup water

1 ripe pear, cored and chopped

1 tablespoon agave nectar

3 cups raw almonds

⅓ cup raw honey

3 tablespoons canola oil

Pinch of salt

1½ cups mashed banana

2 cups fresh strawberries, sliced

1. Place the cashews in a food processor and blend into a fine powder.

2. Add the water and blend again until smooth.

3. Blend in the pear and agave nectar until smooth and set aside.

4. Place the almonds in the food processor and blend into flour.

5. Add the honey, canola oil, and salt and then blend again.

6. Press half of the almond mixture into the bottom of a cake dish, spreading evenly by hand.

7. Spread half the mashed banana on top and top with 1 cup of sliced strawberries.

8. Top the strawberries with the other half of the almond mixture and top with the remaining bananas and the 1 cup of strawberries.

9. Spread the reserved cashew cream over the top of the cake to serve.

Per Serving Calories 1117; Total fat: 80g; Saturated fat: 7g; Total carbs: 86g; Fiber: 19g; Cholesterol: 0mg; Protein: 30g

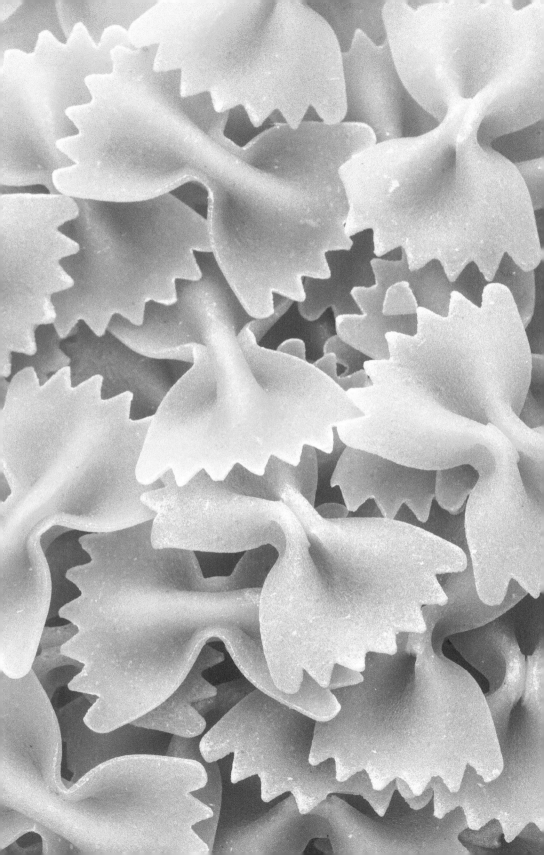

THIRTEEN

Main Dishes

For many people, dinner is the largest meal of the day. No matter when you eat your main meal, the recipes in this chapter are sure to fill you up. From classics like Veggie Fried Rice and Baked Ratatouille to meat-free versions of traditional recipes like Shepherd's Pie and Chicken Parmesan, there is something for everyone here.

RECILES

Vegetarian Black Bean Chili

Serves 6 to 8 • Serving size = about 1 cup

Your favorite chili can be just as satisfying without any meat at all. Substituting black beans for ground beef will do more than just make this meal vegetarian-friendly—it will also make it higher in dietary fiber.

2 tablespoons olive oil

1 tablespoon minced garlic

3 tablespoons chili powder

¾ teaspoon dried oregano

½ teaspoon salt

Pinch of cayenne (optional)

1 red onion, diced

1 red bell pepper, diced

1 yellow squash, chopped

One 14.5-ounce can Italian stewed tomatoes

One 15-ounce can black beans, rinsed and drained

1 cup frozen corn, thawed

1. Heat the olive oil in a Dutch oven over medium heat.

2. Stir in the garlic, chili powder, oregano, salt, and cayenne; cook for 1 minute or until fragrant.

3. Add the onion and red pepper and cook until tender, about 5 minutes.

4. Stir in the yellow squash and stewed tomatoes; bring to a simmer.

5. Simmer the mixture for about 15 minutes until the vegetables are tender.

6. Add the black beans and corn, stirring well to incorporate.

7. Simmer for 5 minutes until heated through; serve hot.

Per Serving Calories 193; Total fat: 6g; Saturated fat: 1g; Total carbs: 31g; Fiber: 9g; Cholesterol: 0mg; Protein: 8g

Greek Pasta Salad

Serves 6 to 8 • Serving size = about 1 cup

This Greek pasta salad is full of Mediterranean flavor. From the sliced olives to the feta cheese crumbles, this recipe is a quick trip to Greece.

One 12- to 16-ounce box rotini pasta

¼ cup diced red onion

¼ cup diced green pepper

¼ cup sliced black olives

1 cup feta cheese crumbles

¼ cup fresh basil leaves, chopped

2 tablespoons extra-virgin olive oil

1 tablespoon red wine vinegar

1 teaspoon dried oregano

Pinch of salt and freshly ground pepper

1. Bring a large pot of water to a boil and add the pasta.

2. Cook the pasta to al dente according to the directions.

3. Rinse the pasta in cool water; drain and transfer it to a large bowl.

4. Stir in the red onion, green pepper, olives, feta, and basil leaves.

5. Whisk together the remaining ingredients and add to the bowl.

6. Toss to coat and chill until ready to serve.

Per Serving Calories 617; Total fat: 16g; Saturated fat: 3g; Total carbs: 97g; Fiber: 22g; Cholesterol: 3mg; Protein: 25g

Fresh Veggie Wrap

Serves 1

This recipe is the perfect way to utilize fresh produce and home-made hummus. Simply spread a tablespoon or so of hummus down the center of a tortilla and top with your favorite chopped veggies!

1 large flour tortilla

1 tablespoon fresh hummus

3 to 4 leaves romaine lettuce

1 small carrot, grated

1 scallion, sliced

¼ green bell pepper, thinly sliced

¼ red bell pepper, thinly sliced

1. Lay the tortilla flat on a plate and spread the hummus evenly over it.

2. Tear the lettuce leaves by hand and arrange them down center of the wrap.

3. Sprinkle the carrots and scallions over the lettuce leaves.

4. Place the peppers on top of the carrots and scallions.

5. Fold up the bottom of the wrap to contain the ingredients and then roll it up and enjoy.

Per Serving Calories 126; Total fat: 2g; Saturated fat: 0g; Total carbs: 26g; Fiber: 5g; Cholesterol: 0mg; Protein: 4g

Barbecue Veggie Sandwich

Serves 4 • Serving size = 1 sandwich

These barbecue veggie sandwiches are perfect for a summer barbecue; they are also a great option to share with friends and family!

1 tablespoon olive oil

1 small red pepper, thinly sliced

8 ounces tempeh, thinly sliced

1 cup vegetarian barbecue sauce

4 toasted sandwich buns

1. Heat the oil in a skillet over medium heat.

2. Add the sliced red pepper and cook for 2 minutes.

3. Stir in the sliced tempeh and cook for 4 to 5 minutes until hot.

4. Add the barbecue sauce and stir well; cook until heated through.

5. Spoon the mixture onto sandwich buns to serve.

Per Serving Calories 363; Total fat: 12g; Saturated fat: 2g; Total carbs: 55g; Fiber: 2g; Cholesterol: 0mg; Protein: 15g

Herbed Lentil Quinoa Burgers

Serves 4 • Serving size = 1 burger

If you miss the feeling of sinking your teeth into a juicy burger, these herbed lentil quinoa burgers will satisfy your hunger. Serve them on whole-grain buns with your favorite burger toppings.

One 15-ounce can red lentils, drained and rinsed

1 cup cooked quinoa

1 small carrot, finely shredded

½ red bell pepper, finely minced

1 scallion, white and green parts, finely chopped

2 tablespoons fresh chopped cilantro leaves

2 tablespoons fresh chopped parsley

¼ teaspoon salt

Freshly ground black pepper

½ cup cornmeal

2 tablespoons olive oil

1. Pulse the red lentils and quinoa in a food processor until moist and the mixture holds together when pressed. If the mixture is too dry, add 1 tablespoon water.

2. Transfer the mixture to a medium bowl and stir in the carrot, red bell pepper, scallion, cilantro, parsley, salt, and pepper.

3. Shape the mixture into 4 burgers; set aside in the refrigerator for 1 hour to firm up.

4. Spread the cornmeal in a shallow dish and dredge the burgers in the cornmeal to coat.

5. Place a large nonstick skillet over medium heat and add the olive oil.

6. Cook the burgers until golden, about 5 minutes per side.

7. Serve on whole-grain buns with your favorite toppings.

Per Serving Calories 282; Total fat: 9g; Saturated fat: 1g; Total carbs: 42g; Fiber: 10g; Cholesterol: 0mg; Protein: 12g

Broccoli Casserole

Serves 6 to 8 • Serving size = about ¾ cup

Not only is this broccoli casserole easy to prepare, but it is something the whole family will love—even your kids!

2½ cups eggless noodles

1¼ cups water

2 cups fresh chopped broccoli florets

1 medium sweet potato, peeled and chopped

1 small carrot, peeled and diced

¼ cup yellow onion, diced

1 teaspoon minced garlic

¼ cup olive oil

¼ cup raw cashew halves

1 tablespoon fresh lemon juice

Salt and pepper

1. Bring a pot of salted water to a boil and add the noodles.

2. Cook the noodles to al dente according to the directions on the box; drain and set aside.

3. Preheat oven to 350°F and grease a 2-quart baking dish with cooking spray.

4. Stir together the water, broccoli, sweet potato, carrot, onion, and garlic in a medium saucepan.

5. Bring the mixture to a boil and then reduce the heat and simmer for 8 to 10 minutes until the vegetables are tender.

6. Transfer the vegetables to a blender and add the olive oil, cashews, lemon juice, salt, and pepper.

7. Blend the mixture until smooth and stir into the cooked pasta.

8. Transfer the mixture to the prepared baking dish and bake for 25 to 30 minutes until hot and bubbling.

Per Serving Calories 216; Total fat: 12g; Saturated fat: 2g; Total carbs: 24g; Fiber: 3g; Cholesterol: 13mg; Protein: 5g

Baked Corn Fritters

Serves 4 to 6

Made with sweet corn and whole-wheat flour, these corn fritters are flavorful and healthy! What more could you ask for?

2 tablespoons olive oil, divided

1 cup frozen sweet corn, thawed

½ cup whole-wheat flour

¾ teaspoon baking powder

⅛ teaspoon salt

½ cup unsweetened almond milk

1 tablespoon apple cider vinegar

3 tablespoons fresh chopped chives

Freshly ground pepper

1. Preheat oven to 350°F and line a baking sheet with foil.

2. Heat 1 tablespoon of oil in a heavy skillet and then add the corn.

3. Cook the corn for 2 to 3 minutes until heated through.

4. Whisk together the flour, baking powder, and salt in a mixing bowl.

5. Beat in the almond milk, cider vinegar, and chives; then stir in the cooked corn.

6. Season with pepper.

7. Add the remaining 1 tablespoon of oil to the skillet and reheat it over medium-high heat.

8. Spoon the corn mixture into the skillet by the heaping tablespoon, leaving at least 1 inch between the fritters.

9. Cook for 2 to 3 minutes per side until lightly browned.

10. Transfer the fritters to the baking sheet and bake for 5 to 10 minutes until crisp. Drain on paper towels and serve hot.

Per Serving Calories 114; Total fat: 8g; Saturated fat: 1g; Total carbs: 11g; Fiber: 2g; Cholesterol: 0mg; Protein: 2g

Salsa-Stuffed Zucchini Boats

Serves 2

This recipe is the perfect way to utilize fresh produce from your local farmers' market or your own garden. Customize this recipe as you see fit, adding a sprinkle of shredded Cheddar or grated Parmesan cheese on top.

1 medium zucchini

1 to 2 tablespoons olive oil

1 ripe tomato, diced

½ small red onion, diced

3 tablespoons fresh chopped cilantro

3 tablespoons fresh chopped basil

Salt and pepper

¼ cup plain bread crumbs

1. Preheat oven to 350°F and line a small baking sheet with parchment paper.

2. Cut the zucchini in half lengthwise using a sharp knife.

3. Using a spoon, carefully scoop out the middle of each zucchini half, leaving a border about ¼ inch thick on the sides and bottom.

4. Chop the zucchini you scooped out and transfer it to a bowl.

5. Brush the zucchini halves lightly with olive oil and place them cut side down on the baking sheet.

6. Bake for 8 to 10 minutes until tender.

7. Stir the tomatoes, onion, cilantro, basil, salt, and pepper into the chopped zucchini.

8. Spoon the mixture into the zucchini boats and sprinkle with bread crumbs.

9. Bake for 5 to 7 minutes until the filling is hot.

Per Serving Calories 209; Total fat: 15g; Saturated fat: 2g; Total carbs: 17g; Fiber: 3g; Cholesterol: 0mg; Protein: 4g

Stuffed Italian Baked Tomatoes

Serves 4

These Italian baked tomatoes are unique and flavorful, the perfect combination if you are looking for a recipe to shake you out of a funk. If you are tired of the same old recipes, these baked tomatoes will wake you up.

4 large ripe tomatoes

¼ cup vegetable broth or water

¼ cup dry couscous

Pinch of salt

2 tablespoons olive oil

3 tablespoons plain bread crumbs

2 teaspoons dried Italian seasoning

1 teaspoon minced garlic

1. Preheat oven to 350°F and lightly grease a glass baking dish.

2. Slice the tops off the tomatoes and carefully scoop out the seeds. Set the tops aside.

3. Arrange the tomatoes cut side down on paper towels to drain.

4. Bring the vegetable broth or water to a boil in a small saucepan and then remove from heat.

5. Immediately stir in couscous and salt; cover the saucepan and set aside.

6. Let the couscous sit for 10 minutes or until it has absorbed the liquid.

7. Place the couscous in a bowl and stir in the remaining ingredients.

8. Spoon the couscous mixture into the tomatoes and place the tomatoes in the prepared baking dish.

9. Place the tops on the tomatoes and bake for 20 to 30 minutes until the tomatoes are tender and the filling is heated through.

Per Serving Calories 155; Total fat: 8g; Saturated fat: 1g; Total carbs: 19g; Fiber: 3g; Cholesterol: 0mg; Protein: 4g

Spaghetti Squash with Sautéed Veggies

Serves 6 • Serving size = about 1 cup

Spaghetti squash is low in calories but high in nutrients. It is a good source of dietary fiber and healthy carbohydrates.

1 large spaghetti squash

2 tablespoons olive oil

1 jalapeño, seeded and minced

1 teaspoon fresh grated ginger

1 teaspoon minced garlic

1 yellow onion, chopped

1 green bell pepper, chopped

1 red bell pepper, chopped

1 cup diced tomatoes

Salt

Pinch of cayenne pepper

1. Preheat oven to 350°F.

2. Cut the spaghetti squash in half with a sharp knife.

3. Scoop out the seeds and place the squash halves cut side down in a lightly greased glass baking dish.

4. Bake the squash for 30 minutes or until a sharp knife inserted into the skin of the squash slides in easily.

5. Remove the dish from the oven and set aside until the squash is cool enough to handle.

6. Meanwhile, heat the oil in a heavy skillet.

7. Stir in the jalapeño, ginger, and garlic. Cook for 1 minute.

8. Add the onion and bell peppers and cook for 4 to 6 minutes until tender.

9. Stir in the diced tomatoes and cook for 2 minutes longer.

10. Using a fork, shred the cooked squash and add it to the skillet with the vegetables.

11. Season with salt and cayenne pepper and cook until heated through.

Per Serving Calories 99; Total fat: 6g; Saturated fat: 1g; Total carbs: 13g; Fiber: 1g; Cholesterol: 0mg; Protein: 2g

Pasta with Mushrooms

Serves 4 to 6 • Serving size = about 1 cup

Mushrooms are a good source of selenium, which helps to promote bladder health. Mushrooms are also one of the only foods that naturally produce vitamin D when exposed to sunlight.

One 16-ounce box penne pasta

3 tablespoons olive oil, divided

1 teaspoon minced garlic

2 cups sliced mushrooms

¾ cup vegan white wine, divided

Salt and pepper

½ cup chopped yellow onion

One 14-ounce can artichokes, drained and sliced

2 tablespoons fresh chopped thyme

Fresh parsley for garnishing

1. Bring a large pot of salted water to a boil and add the pasta.

2. Cook to al dente according to the directions, about 8 minutes.

3. Meanwhile, heat 1½ tablespoons of oil in a heavy skillet over medium heat.

4. Add the garlic and cook for 1 minute.

5. Stir in the mushrooms until coated with oil.

6. Stir in ¼ cup of white wine and cook until most of the liquid has evaporated.

7. Remove from the heat and season with salt and pepper.

8. Heat the remaining oil in another skillet over medium heat.

9. Stir in the onion and cook for 3 to 5 minutes. Add the artichokes and stir well.

➜

10. Stir in the remaining wine and fresh thyme; then cook until most of the liquid has been absorbed.

11. Spoon the mushroom and artichoke mixture into a serving bowl.

12. Drain the cooked pasta and add to the bowl with the mushroom and artichoke mixture.

13. Toss to combine and serve garnished with fresh parsley.

Per Serving Calories 575; Total fat: 15g; Saturated fat: 2g; Total carbs: 82g; Fiber: 10g; Cholesterol: 0mg; Protein: 18g

Garlic Green Pepper Pasta

Serves 6 to 8 • Serving size = about 1 cup

This recipe is the perfect combination of pasta and crunchy green peppers. Serve it up for a family dinner or share it at your next community picnic.

One 16-ounce box rotini pasta

1½ tablespoons olive oil

1 tablespoon minced garlic

2 green bell peppers, thinly sliced

½ yellow onion, chopped

Salt and pepper

1. Bring a large pot of water to a boil and add the pasta.

2. Cook the pasta to al dente according to the directions; then drain and set aside.

3. Heat the oil in a large skillet over medium heat.

4. Add the garlic and cook for 1 minute.

5. Stir in the peppers and onion and then cook for 5 to 6 minutes until tender.

6. Add the cooked pasta and toss to combine.

7. Season the pasta with salt and pepper; cook until heated through. Serve hot.

Per Serving Calories 328; Total fat: 5g; Saturated fat: 1g; Total carbs: 60g; Fiber: 3g; Cholesterol: 0mg; Protein: 10g

Penne with Artichokes

Serves 4 to 6 • Serving size = about 1 cup

Artichokes are high in antioxidants, which help to repair cellular damage caused by free radicals; they also help to reduce your risk for cancer.

One 16-ounce box penne pasta

3 tablespoons olive oil, divided

1 teaspoon minced garlic

¾ cup dry white wine, divided

Salt and pepper

½ cup chopped yellow onion

One 14-ounce can artichokes, drained and sliced

2 tablespoons fresh chopped thyme

Fresh parsley for garnishing

1. Bring a large pot of salted water to boil and add the pasta.

2. Cook to al dente according to the directions, about 8 minutes.

3. Meanwhile, heat 1½ tablespoons of oil in a heavy skillet over medium heat.

4. Add the garlic and cook for 1 minute.

5. Stir in ¼ cup white wine and cook until most of the liquid has evaporated.

6. Remove from heat and season with salt and pepper.

7. Heat the remaining oil in another skillet over medium heat.

8. Stir in the onion and cook for 3 to 5 minutes.

9. Add the sliced artichokes and stir well.

10. Stir in the garlic and wine mixture, remaining wine, and fresh thyme and cook until most of the liquid has been absorbed.

11. Spoon the artichoke mixture into a serving bowl.

12. Drain the cooked pasta and add to the bowl with the artichoke mixture.

13. Toss to combine; serve garnished with fresh parsley.

Per Serving Calories 607; Total fat: 13g; Saturated fat: 2g; Total carbs: 100g; Fiber: 12g; Cholesterol: 0mg; Protein: 18g

Zucchini with Lemon Garlic Pasta

Serves 6 to 8 • Serving size = about 1 cup

Zucchini is an excellent source of iron, magnesium, phosphorus, and copper; it is also a good source of A and B vitamins, which help reduce your risk for cardiovascular disease.

One 16-ounce box linguine

2 tablespoons olive oil

1 tablespoon minced garlic

1 medium zucchini, thinly sliced

¼ cup fresh lemon juice

1 teaspoon cornstarch

Salt and pepper

1. Bring a large pot of water to boil and add the pasta.

2. Cook the pasta to al dente according to the directions and then drain and set aside.

3. Heat the oil in a large skillet over medium heat.

4. Add the garlic and cook for 1 minute.

5. Stir in the sliced zucchini and cook for 3 to 4 minutes until tender.

6. Whisk together the lemon juice and cornstarch; then stir into the skillet and cook for 1 minute until it begins to thicken.

7. Add the cooked pasta and toss to coat.

8. Season the pasta with salt and pepper; then cook until heated through. Serve hot.

Per Serving Calories 502; Total fat: 9g; Saturated fat: 1g; Total carbs: 89g; Fiber: 4g; Cholesterol: 0mg; Protein: 15g

Oven-Baked Risotto

Serves 8 • Serving size = about ½ cup

Risotto is traditionally served hot and creamy, often blended with mushrooms or chopped vegetables. This baked risotto takes half the time to prepare, and you can use the leftovers to make the next recipe in this book, Baked Risotto Cakes.

1 tablespoon canola oil

1 cup chopped onion

1½ cups Arborio rice

4 cups water, divided

1 cup low-sodium vegetable stock

2 teaspoons dried basil

½ teaspoon salt

Pinch of black pepper

1 large carrot, peeled and finely chopped

2 medium zucchini, diced

1 yellow squash, diced

2 tablespoons unsalted butter

½ cup shredded Parmesan cheese

1. Preheat oven to 425°F.

2. Heat the oil in a Dutch oven over medium heat.

3. Stir in the onions and cook for 3 minutes; then add the rice.

4. Cook for 1 minute, stirring, to coat the rice with oil.

5. Whisk in 3 cups water along with the vegetable stock, basil, salt, and pepper.

6. Add the carrot and bring the mixture to a boil.

7. Stir in the zucchini and squash; then cover the Dutch oven and transfer it to the preheated oven.

8. Bake for 25 to 30 minutes, until most of the liquid has been absorbed by the rice, and then remove from the oven.

9. Stir in the remaining 1 cup water, along with the butter and Parmesan cheese, to serve.

Per Serving Calories 113; Total fat: 6g; Saturated fat: 3g; Total carbs: 12g; Fiber: 1g; Cholesterol: 13mg; Protein: 4g

Baked Risotto Cakes

Serving Size = 2 Cakes

These baked risotto cakes are the ideal way to use leftover baked risotto. This recipe is ideal for a quick lunch, or it can be used as a side dish for a main meal.

½ cup plain bread crumbs

½ cup Oven-Baked Risotto (page 198)

¼ cup fresh chopped parsley

1. Preheat oven to 400°F and line a baking sheet with aluminum foil.

2. Spread the bread crumbs in a shallow dish.

3. Shape the baked risotto into balls by hand, using about ¼ cup risotto for each ball.

4. Flatten the balls into patties and press them into the bread crumbs to coat on both sides.

5. Arrange the patties on the prepared baking sheet and bake for 30 minutes or until evenly browned.

6. Serve hot, garnished with fresh parsley.

Per Serving Calories 326; Total fat: 9g; Saturated fat: 4g; Total carbs: 51g; Fiber: 4g; Cholesterol: 13mg; Protein: 11g

Carrot Onion Risotto

Serves 4 to 6 • Serving size = about ¾ cup

Carrots are a great source of vitamins and minerals; they contain high levels of vitamin A as well as calcium, potassium, and sodium. Carrots have also been shown to help reduce your risk for cancer and cardiovascular disease.

6½ cups vegetable stock

2 tablespoons olive oil

1 pound fresh carrots, thinly sliced

1 large yellow onion, finely chopped

1½ cups Arborio rice

1 teaspoon minced garlic

Salt and pepper

½ cup vegan white wine

2 tablespoons fresh chopped parsley

1 tablespoon fresh chopped chives

1 teaspoon fresh lemon juice

1. Bring the vegetable stock to a simmer in a large saucepan.

2. In a separate saucepan, heat the oil over medium heat.

3. Stir in the carrots and onion.

4. Cook for 3 to 4 minutes until slightly tender.

5. Stir in the rice and garlic and then season with salt and pepper.

6. Cook for several minutes until the grains of rice begin to crackle and pop.

7. Whisk in the wine and cook until it has almost evaporated.

8. Spoon about ½ cup of the warmed vegetable stock into the saucepan.

9. Cook, stirring, until the liquid is almost absorbed.

10. Keep adding the stock, about ½ cup at a time, after the liquid has been absorbed.

11. Cook the rice for a total of about 20 to 25 minutes, until it is tender but not mushy.

12. Remove the pan from the heat once the rice is tender and stir in another ½ cup of broth along with the parsley, chives, and lemon juice.

13. Ladle into bowls and serve immediately.

Per Serving Calories 176; Total fat: 7g; Saturated fat: 1g; Total carbs: 26g; Fiber: 3g; Cholesterol: 0mg; Protein: 2g

Italian Pasta Bake

Serves 4 to 6 • Serving size = about 1 cup

This Italian pasta bake is a simple but hearty meal—easy to prepare and filling enough to feed the whole family. Feel free to customize this recipe using your favorite meat substitute or no meat at all.

8 ounces penne pasta

One 28-ounce can crushed tomatoes

1 tablespoon olive oil

1 tablespoon minced garlic

1 cup meat-free crumbles

2 tablespoons tomato paste

2 tablespoons fresh chopped basil

Salt and pepper

1½ cups shredded mozzarella cheese

1. Preheat oven to 350°F.

2. Bring a large pot of salted water to a boil and add the penne pasta.

3. Cool for 7 to 9 minutes until tender; then drain and set aside.

4. Pour the crushed tomatoes into a food processor and blend until smooth.

5. Heat the oil in a large skillet over medium heat.

6. Add the garlic and cook for 1 minute.

7. Stir in the puréed tomatoes, meat-free crumbles, tomato paste, basil, salt, and pepper.

8. Lower heat and simmer for about 10 minutes until the sauce is thickened.

9. Stir in the cooked pasta and half the cheese.

10. Pour the mixture into a lightly greased casserole dish and sprinkle with the remaining cheese.

11. Cover with foil and bake for 15 minutes.

12. Remove the foil and bake for an additional 10 minutes until the cheese is melted.

Per Serving Calories 464; Total fat: 15g; Saturated fat: 6g; Total carbs: 61g; Fiber: 7g; Cholesterol: 33mg; Protein: 24g

Baked Eggplant Parmesan

Serves 4 • Serving size = 4 eggplant slices

Eggplant Parmesan is a great meat-free alternative to an Italian classic. This version is easy to prepare and something the whole family will love.

1 pound eggplant

1 teaspoon kosher salt

1 cup skim milk

¾ cup all-purpose flour

1 teaspoon dried oregano

1 teaspoon dried thyme

2 cups plain bread crumbs

1. Preheat oven to 450°F and line a baking sheet with parchment paper.

2. Peel the eggplant carefully with a sharp knife and cut it into ¼-inch slices.

3. Arrange the slices on paper towels and sprinkle with salt.

4. Let the eggplant sit for about 20 minutes and then pat dry with a paper towel or clean cloth.

5. Whisk together the milk, flour, oregano, and thyme; pour into a shallow dish.

6. Dip the eggplant slices in the milk mixture and then coat with bread crumbs.

7. Spread out the breaded eggplant slices on the prepared baking sheet and bake for 6 to 8 minutes per side until crisp and browned.

8. Serve the cooked eggplant hot over a bed of pasta with pasta sauce.

Per Serving Calories 193; Total fat: 1g; Saturated fat: 0g; Total carbs: 38g; Fiber: 5g; Cholesterol: 1mg; Protein: 8g

Spinach Parmesan Stuffed Shells

Serves 6 • Serving size = about 6 stuffed shells

These shells are stuffed with a creamy blend of ricotta and mozzarella cheese along with spinach. Spinach is high in calcium, potassium, and protein; it has also been shown to support healthy cognitive function.

1 box jumbo shell pasta

1 cup part-skim ricotta cheese

½ cup shredded mozzarella cheese

½ tablespoon olive oil

2 teaspoons minced garlic

1 medium vidalia onion, diced

1 cup fresh baby spinach leaves, chopped

½ cup fresh basil leaves, chopped

2 tablespoons grated Parmesan cheese

1 tablespoon fresh lemon juice

Salt and pepper

3 cups pasta sauce

1. Bring a large pot of water to boil and add the shells.

2. Cook the pasta to al dente according to the directions; drain and set aside.

3. Combine the ricotta and mozzarella in a food processor and blend until smooth.

4. Heat the oil in a skillet over medium heat.

5. Add the garlic and onion and cook for about 5 minutes until softened.

6. Stir in the spinach and basil and cook for another 2 to 3 minutes.

7. Spoon the blended ricotta into the skillet and whisk in the Parmesan cheese, lemon juice, salt, and pepper.

8. Cook the mixture for 8 to 10 minutes until most of the liquid has cooked off.

9. Spoon 1 cup of pasta sauce into the prepared dish and spread evenly.

10. Spoon 1½ to 2 tablespoons of the cheese mixture into each cooked shell and arrange the shells in the prepared dish.

11. Pour the rest of the pasta sauce over the shells and cover the dish with foil.

12. Poke several holes in the foil to vent steam and bake for 20 minutes or until heated through.

13. Let sit for 10 minutes, covered, before serving.

Per Serving Calories 368; Total fat: 11g; Saturated fat: 5g; Total carbs: 51g; Fiber: 5g; Cholesterol: 25mg; Protein: 15g

Baked Ratatouille

Serves 6 • Serving size = about 1 cup

Ratatouille is a traditional French dish made with stewed vegetables. In this recipe, zucchini, yellow squash, and eggplant are the stars, flavored with garlic and fresh basil.

1 medium zucchini

1 medium yellow summer squash

1 pound eggplant

1 pound ripe red tomatoes

1 tablespoon minced garlic

2 tablespoons fresh chopped basil

Couscous, for serving

1. Preheat oven to 250°F.

2. Rinse the vegetables well and trim off the stems as needed.

3. Slice the vegetables thick, about ½ inch for each slice.

4. Lightly grease a round casserole dish with cooking spray and arrange a layer of zucchini slices on the bottom.

5. Top with layers of squash, eggplant, and tomato.

6. Sprinkle the garlic and basil on top of the casserole and bake, covered, for 1 to 1½ hours until the vegetables are tender.

7. Serve hot over a bed of fresh couscous.

Per Serving Calories 32; Total fat: 0g; Saturated fat: 0g; Total carbs: 7g; Fiber: 4g; Cholesterol: 0mg; Protein: 2g

Tomato Onion Barbecue Quesadillas

Serves 1

These barbecue quesadillas are a great option for either lunch or dinner. Easy to prepare and full of flavor, they are sure to be a hit with kids and adults alike.

1½ tablespoons olive oil

1 garlic clove, minced

1 small onion, thinly sliced

1 small tomato, diced

One 8-inch whole-wheat tortilla

1½ tablespoons barbecue sauce

Cooking spray

1. Heat the olive oil in a small skillet over medium heat.

2. Add the garlic and cook for 1 minute.

3. Stir in the onions and toss to coat with oil.

4. Reduce the heat to medium-low and cook the onions until caramelized, about 12 to 15 minutes.

5. Stir in the tomato and cook for 2 minutes.

6. Spoon the barbecue sauce onto the tortilla and spread evenly.

7. Spoon the onion, tomato, and garlic mixture onto half of the tortilla and fold the empty half over top.

8. Lightly spray the top of the quesadilla with cooking spray and place it in the skillet, flipping it so the sprayed side is down.

9. Cook for 1 to 2 minutes until the tortilla is browned.

10. Spray the top of the tortilla with cooking spray and then carefully flip it and cook until browned on the other side.

11. Cut into 2 pieces to serve.

Per Serving Calories 330; Total fat: 22g; Saturated fat: 3g; Total carbs: 32g; Fiber: 5g; Cholesterol: 0mg; Protein: 4g

Mexican Rice and Bean Burritos

Serves 4 • Serving size = 2 corn tortillas, ½ cup refried beans

If you are looking for a quick and easy recipe to serve up for dinner, try these Mexican rice and bean burritos. These burritos are sure to be a hit with the whole family—even picky eaters!

8 yellow corn tortillas

2 cups refried beans

1½ cups cooked Mexican rice

Fresh salsa or guacamole

1. Wrap the tortillas in paper towel, two at a time, and microwave on high heat for 5 to 8 seconds until warmed.

2. Spoon about ¼ cup refried beans down the center of each tortilla.

3. Top the beans with about 2 tablespoons Mexican rice.

4. Roll the tortillas up around the filling and serve with salsa and guacamole.

Per Serving Calories 357; Total fat: 4g; Saturated fat: 1g; Total carbs: 69g; Fiber: 12g; Cholesterol: 10mg; Protein: 14g

Black Bean and Corn Enchiladas

Serves 6 • Serving size = about 1 cup

If you are a fan of Mexican food, these black bean and corn enchiladas are sure to hit the spot. Feel free to add some minced jalapeño to give them a little heat.

½ tablespoon olive oil

1 garlic clove, minced

1 yellow onion, chopped

1 green bell pepper, chopped

1 red bell pepper, chopped

One 15-ounce can black beans, rinsed and drained

½ cup frozen corn, thawed

2 tablespoons taco seasoning

6 large whole-wheat tortillas, warmed

½ cup enchilada sauce

1. Heat the oil in a heavy skillet over medium heat.

2. Add the garlic and cook for 1 minute.

3. Stir in the onion and bell peppers. Cook, stirring, for 5 to 7 minutes.

4. Stir in the black beans, corn, and taco seasoning.

5. Cook the mixture for 2 to 3 minutes or until heated through.

6. Spoon about ½ cup of the black bean vegetable mixture down the center of each whole-wheat tortilla.

7. Roll the tortillas up around the filling and place in a greased baking dish.

8. After placing all the tortillas in the dish, top with enchilada sauce.

9. Bake the enchiladas for 25 to 30 minutes, or until hot and bubbling.

Per Serving Calories 203; Total fat: 3g; Saturated fat: 1g; Total carbs: 37g; Fiber: 8g; Cholesterol: 0mg; Protein: 8g

Bean and Rice Casserole

Serves 4 to 6 • Serving size = about 1 cup

This baked bean and rice casserole is sure to satisfy your hunger. Hot and hearty, it is the ideal meal for a hungry family.

2 vegetarian soy sausages

Two 15-ounce cans vegetarian baked beans

1 teaspoon chili powder

½ teaspoon red pepper flakes

2 cups steamed white rice

½ cup plain bread crumbs

2 tablespoons unsalted butter, melted

Salt and pepper

1. Preheat oven to 375°F and lightly grease a 2-quart casserole dish.

2. Cut the sausages into ½-inch slices and cut each slice in half. Set aside.

3. Pour the baked beans into the casserole dish and stir in the veggie sausages, chili powder, and red pepper flakes.

4. Stir in the steamed rice and then sprinkle the mixture with bread crumbs.

5. Drizzle the melted butter over the bread crumbs and season with salt and pepper.

6. Bake for 25 minutes or until heated through; then increase the oven temperature to 500°F.

7. Bake for 2 to 3 minutes to brown the topping, and cool for 5 minutes before serving.

Per Serving Calories 387; Total fat: 9g; Saturated fat: 4g; Total carbs: 64g; Fiber: 6g; Cholesterol: 15mg; Protein: 14g

Shepherd's Pie

Serves 4 to 6 • Serving size = about 1 cup

Also known as cottage pie, shepherd's pie is a classic recipe that has been around since the late 1800s. The recipe originated in Ireland, traditionally made with lamb, but this version is completely meat-free and vegetarian-friendly.

1 tablespoon olive oil

1 large yellow onion, diced

1 cup organic vegetable stock

12 ounces meat-free crumbles

1½ cups frozen mixed vegetables, thawed

Salt and pepper

2 cups prepared mashed potatoes

1½ cups shredded cheddar cheese

1. Preheat oven to 375°F and lightly grease a 2-quart casserole dish with cooking spray.

2. Heat the oil in a large skillet over medium heat.

3. Stir in the onion and cook for 3 to 5 minutes until slightly softened.

4. Stir in the vegetable stock and cook for an additional 3 minutes.

5. Add the meat-free crumbles and then reduce the heat and simmer for 10 minutes.

6. Stir in the thawed vegetables and cook until heated through, about 5 minutes. Season with salt and pepper.

7. Spoon the mixture into the prepared dish and top with prepared mashed potatoes.

8. Sprinkle evenly with cheese and bake for 25 minutes, or until the cheese is melted.

Per Serving Calories 443; Total fat: 25g; Saturated fat: 11g; Total carbs: 31g; Fiber: 6g; Cholesterol: 46mg; Protein: 29g

Sesame Tofu Noodles

Serves 4 to 6 • Serving size = about 1 cup

These sesame tofu noodles are a delicious combination of peanut, soy, and sesame flavor. Enjoy them hot for dinner or serve them chilled for a refreshing lunch.

10 ounces brown rice noodles

6 cups boiling water

4 scallions, chopped

⅓ cup smooth peanut butter

¼ cup sesame oil

3 tablespoons soy sauce

1½ tablespoons tahini sauce

1 tablespoon granulated sugar

1 tablespoon olive oil

8 ounces firm tofu, cubed

1 medium cucumber, peeled into strips

1. Place the rice noodles in a bowl and pour the boiling water over them.

2. Let the noodles sit for 20 minutes or until they are soft, according to the directions on the package.

3. Drain the noodles and transfer them to a serving bowl.

4. Whisk together the scallions, peanut butter, sesame oil, soy sauce, tahini, and granulated sugar in a bowl.

5. Pour about two-thirds of the sauce over the noodles and stir well.

6. Heat the oil in a skillet over medium-high heat.

7. Add the cubed tofu and cook for 4 to 6 minutes, stirring often, until browned on the outside.

8. Stir the tofu into the noodles and toss to coat.

9. Arrange the peeled cucumber around the edges of the bowl and drizzle with the remaining sauce to serve.

Per Serving Calories 685; Total fat: 38g; Saturated fat: 6g; Total carbs: 74g; Fiber: 5g; Cholesterol: 0mg; Protein: 17g

Veggie Fried Rice

Serves 6 • Serving size = about ¾ cup

This veggie fried rice works equally well as a side dish and as a main entrée. Make up a big batch of fried rice and keep it in the refrigerator to enjoy all week long.

½ cup textured vegetable protein

½ cup water

2½ tablespoons soy sauce, divided

2 tablespoons olive oil

1 teaspoon minced garlic

1 cup chopped yellow onions

1 cup chopped carrots

1 cup chopped mushrooms

¼ cup chopped celery

3 cups brown rice, cooked

¼ teaspoon ground ginger

¼ teaspoon black pepper

1. Combine the textured vegetable protein, water, and 1 tablespoon soy sauce in a bowl.

2. Stir well and set aside for about 5 minutes until the liquid is absorbed.

3. Heat the oil in a heavy skillet over medium heat.

4. Add the garlic and cook for 1 minute.

5. Stir in the onions, carrots, mushrooms, and celery.

6. Cook for 3 to 4 minutes until the onions begin to soften.

7. Move the vegetables to the sides of the skillet and stir in the textured vegetable protein.

8. Add the remaining soy sauce then stir in the cooked rice.

9. Stir in the ground ginger and black pepper, stirring well to coat the rice with sauce.

10. Remove from heat and set aside for 3 to 5 minutes before serving.

Per Serving Calories 198; Total fat: 5g; Saturated fat: 1g; Total carbs: 23g; Fiber: 3g; Cholesterol: 0mg; Protein: 18g

Chickpea Curry

Serves 3 to 4 • Serving size = about 1 cup

Chickpeas are a great source of dietary fiber and vegetarian protein. They are rich in manganese, which helps your body maintain healthy energy production.

2 tablespoons olive oil

1 large yellow onion, thinly sliced

1 tablespoon minced garlic

1 tablespoon curry powder

One 14-ounce can light coconut milk

One 14-ounce can chickpeas, rinsed and drained

2 large bell peppers, cut into 2-inch chunks

2 tablespoons tomato paste

1 tablespoon brown sugar, packed

1 tablespoon fresh lemon juice

Salt and pepper

2 tablespoons fresh chopped parsley

1. Heat the oil in a large skillet over medium heat.

2. Stir in the onion and cook for 3 to 5 minutes until just softened.

3. Add the garlic and curry powder and cook for 1 minute, stirring often.

4. Stir in the remaining ingredients, aside from the parsley, and bring the mixture to a boil.

5. Reduce the heat and simmer for 20 to 25 minutes until the vegetables are tender and the sauce thickens.

6. Serve hot, garnished with fresh chopped parsley.

Per Serving Calories 487; Total fat: 24g; Saturated fat: 9g; Total carbs: 59g; Fiber: 11g; Cholesterol: 0mg; Protein: 11g

Vegetable Tofu Curry

Serves 4 to 6 • Serving size = about 1 cup

This vegetable tofu curry is hot and hearty with a little bit of ethnic flair. Feel free to use whatever vegetables you have on hand or stop by your local farmers' market for fresh produce.

½ tablespoon olive oil

1 medium onion, chopped

1 red bell pepper, chopped

2 teaspoons curry powder

½ teaspoon ground ginger

2 cups chopped broccoli

2 cups chopped cauliflower

1 cup chopped carrots

1 cup organic vegetable stock

One 14-ounce can chickpeas, rinsed and drained

One 10-ounce box firm tofu, cubed

½ cup whole milk

3 tablespoons shredded coconut, unsweetened

Salt and pepper

1. Heat the oil in a large skillet over medium heat.

2. Stir in the onion and cook for 5 minutes until just softened.

3. Add the bell pepper, curry powder, and ginger and cook for 1 minute.

4. Stir in the broccoli, cauliflower, carrots, and vegetable stock.

5. Cook for 4 to 5 minutes and then reduce the heat and simmer, covered, for 10 minutes.

6. Add the chickpeas and tofu; then increase the heat to bring the mixture to a simmer.

7. Cook for an additional 10 minutes, covered, and then stir in the whole milk and coconut.

8. Season with salt and pepper before serving.

Per Serving Calories 297; Total fat: 8g; Saturated fat: 2g; Total carbs: 45g; Fiber: 10g; Cholesterol: 3mg; Protein: 15g

FOURTEEN

Sweet Treats and Snacks

Luckily, most desserts do not include meat anyway, so it isn't much of a challenge to make them vegetarian! In this chapter you will find a collection of delectable desserts made from all kinds of vegetarian-friendly ingredients. From Vanilla Bean Cupcakes to Creamy Chocolate Mousse, these recipes are sure to make your mouth water.

RECImPES

Baked Apple Chips

Serves 3 to 4

If you are looking for a sweet and simple dessert that won't undo your day, try these baked apple chips. Made with nothing more than apples, cinnamon, and a pinch of sugar, they are a guilt-free treat.

4 ripe Gala apples

1 tablespoon ground cinnamon

1 teaspoon sugar

1. Preheat oven to 325°F and line a standard baking sheet with parchment paper.

2. Rinse the apples and remove the cores.

3. Slice the apples as thin as possible and place them in a mixing bowl.

4. Add the cinnamon and sugar and toss the apple slices to coat.

5. Arrange the apple slices on the baking sheet and bake for 30 minutes.

6. Carefully flip the slices and cook them for another 35 to 45 minutes, or until the moisture has baked out.

7. Turn off the oven and let the apple chips sit until crisp. Store in an airtight container.

Per Serving Calories 165; Total fat: 1g; Saturated fat: 0g; Total carbs: 44g; Fiber: 8g; Cholesterol: 0mg; Protein: 1g

Cinnamon Applesauce

Makes about 2 cups • Serving size = about ½ cup

Knowing how to make your own applesauce at home is bound to come in handy, whether you have a houseful of kids or like to have a bit of something sweet from time to time. This applesauce takes only a few minutes to make, and you can use whatever kind of apples you have on hand.

4 sweet apples, peeled and cored

1 tablespoon light brown sugar

Pinch ground cinnamon or nutmeg

1. Coarsely chop the apples and place them in a microwave-safe bowl.

2. Cover the bowl with plastic wrap and microwave on high power for 1 minute.

3. Stir the apples and then microwave for 3 minutes more or until the apples are softened, stirring after each minute.

4. Spoon the mixture into a food processor and blend until smooth.

5. Add the brown sugar and cinnamon; pulse to combine.

6. Serve the applesauce warm, or chill before serving.

Per Serving Calories 125; Total fat: 0g; Saturated fat: 0g; Total carbs: 33g; Fiber: 5g; Cholesterol: 0mg; Protein: 1g

Honey-Glazed Pears

These poached pears are not something you've likely tried before. After your first bite, however, you will find yourself making this recipe as often as you can!

1 ripe pears, halved and seeded

½ cup water

⅓ cup raw honey

1 teaspoon vanilla extract

1 teaspoon almond extract

Pinch ground cloves

1. Peel the pears, if desired, and remove the stem.

2. Combine the remaining ingredients in a small saucepan and bring to a boil.

3. Reduce heat to medium-high and add the pear halves.

4. Cover the saucepan and cook for 5 to 7 minutes or until the pears are tender.

5. Using a slotted spoon, place the pears onto two plates.

6. Continue to simmer the glaze until thickened, and drizzle over the pears to serve.

Per Serving Calories 239; Total fat: 0g; Saturated fat: 0g; Total carbs: 63g; Fiber: 3g; Cholesterol: 0mg; Protein: 1g

Herb Marinated Peaches

This recipe is both vegetarian and raw—it couldn't get any healthier!

¼ cup fresh mint leaves, chopped

1 tablespoon fresh chopped basil

1 tablespoon fresh lemon juice

1 teaspoon raw honey

2 ripe peaches, pitted and chopped

Chopped nuts for garnishing

1. Combine the mint, basil, lemon juice, and honey in a bowl.

2. Add the peaches and stir well. Chill for about 1 hour.

3. Serve cold, garnished with chopped nuts if desired.

Per Serving Calories 77; Total fat: 1g; Saturated fat: 0g; Total carbs: 18g; Fiber: 3g; Cholesterol: 0mg; Protein: 2g

Grilled Peaches with Honey

These grilled peaches are hot and sweet, the perfect combination in a dessert. Glazed with balsamic vinegar and honey, the flavor of these peaches will astound you.

½ cup raw honey

¼ cup balsamic vinegar

½ teaspoon vanilla extract

4 ripe peaches, pitted and halved

1. Whisk together the honey, balsamic vinegar, and vanilla extract in a small bowl.

2. Preheat an indoor grill pan over medium-high heat.

3. Brush half of the balsamic mixture over the peaches and place them on the grill, cut side down.

4. Grill for about 2 minutes and then carefully flip and brush with more glaze.

5. Serve the peaches warm, drizzled with the remaining glaze.

Per Serving Calories 193; Total fat: 0g; Saturated fat: 0g; Total carbs: 49g; Fiber: 2g; Cholesterol: 0mg; Protein: 2g

Fruit Salad with Fresh Mint

Makes about 5½ to 6 cups • Serving size = about 1 cup

This recipe combines the sweetness and tartness of fresh fruit with the coolness of mint—the perfect treat to enjoy by the pool in the summer heat.

2 cups fresh strawberries, halved

1½ cups fresh blueberries

1 cup fresh raspberries

1 cup fresh blackberries

½ cup fresh mint leaves, chopped

2 tablespoons fresh lime juice

1. Combine the berries in a mixing bowl.

2. Add the mint leaves and lime juice; toss to coat.

3. Transfer to a serving bowl and chill before serving, if desired.

Per Serving Calories 75; Total fat: 1g; Saturated fat: 0g; Total carbs: 18g; Fiber: 6g; Cholesterol: 0mg; Protein: 2g

Strawberry Kiwi Freeze Pops

Makes 8 freeze pops • Serving size = 1 fruit pop

If you are in the mood for a sweet and fruity summer treat, try these strawberry kiwi freeze pops! If strawberry and kiwi isn't your ideal flavor combination, don't be afraid to mix and match other fruit flavors.

1 cup water

½ cup superfine sugar

1 teaspoon lemon zest

2 cups fresh strawberries, sliced

2 ripe kiwis, peeled and sliced

8 small paper cups

8 wooden sticks

1. Whisk together the water, sugar, and lemon zest in a small saucepan over medium heat.

2. Cook, stirring often, until the sugar is dissolved.

3. Remove the pan from the heat and set it aside to cool.

4. Combine the strawberries and kiwi in a food processor and blend until puréed.

5. Stir the fruit mixture into the sugar water; then strain through a mesh sieve and discard the solids.

6. Pour the fruit liquid into eight small paper cups and place a wooden stick upright in the center of each cup.

7. Place the cups on a small tray and freeze until solid.

8. Peel away the paper cup to enjoy the freeze pops.

Per Serving Calories 70; Total fat: 0g; Saturated fat: 0g; Total carbs: 18g; Fiber: 1g; Cholesterol: 0mg; Protein: 1g

Strawberry Sorbet

Makes about 6 cups • Serving size = about ½ cup

Nothing is quite as refreshing as a bowl of fresh fruit sorbet on a hot summer evening. Using this simple recipe, you can make your own sorbet at home so you can enjoy it any time of year!

½ cup water

½ cup superfine sugar

2 tablespoons fresh lemon juice

5 cups fresh strawberries

1. Combine the water, sugar, and lemon juice in a medium saucepan over medium heat.

2. Cook, stirring until the sugar has dissolved, and then set the saucepan aside.

3. Place the strawberries in a food processor and pour in the sugar mixture.

4. Blend until smooth. Strain the mixture through a mesh sieve and discard the solids.

5. Pour the strawberry syrup into a shallow dish and freeze until solid.

6. Just before serving, break the strawberry mixture into pieces and blend it in a food processor until smooth.

7. Serve immediately.

Per Serving Calories 51; Total fat: 0g; Saturated fat: 0g; Total carbs: 13g; Fiber: 1g; Cholesterol: 0mg; Protein: 0g

Blueberry Lime Sorbet

Makes about 6 cups • Serving size = about ½ cup

This blueberry lime sorbet is light and refreshing—just the thing you need to cool off on a hot summer night.

½ cup water

½ cup superfine sugar

2 tablespoons fresh lime juice

1 tablespoon lime zest

5 cups fresh blueberries

1. Combine the water, sugar, lime juice, and lime zest in a medium saucepan over medium heat.

2. Cook, stirring until the sugar has dissolved, and then set the saucepan aside.

3. Place the blueberries in a food processor and pour in the sugar mixture.

4. Blend until smooth. Strain the mixture through a mesh sieve and discard the solids.

5. Pour the blueberry syrup into a shallow dish and freeze until solid.

6. Just before serving, break the blueberry mixture into pieces and blend it in a food processor until smooth.

7. Serve immediately.

Per Serving Calories 66; Total fat: 0g; Saturated fat: 0g; Total carbs: 17g; Fiber: 2g; Cholesterol: 0mg; Protein: 1g

Creamy Chocolate Mousse

Made with tofu and light sour cream, this creamy chocolate mousse tastes more sinful than it actually is. Not only is it smooth and delicious, but it is also vegetarian-friendly!

28 ounces soft refrigerated tofu

2 cups semisweet chocolate chips

1 cup cream cheese, at room temperature

½ cup light sour cream

1 cup powdered sugar

1. Drain the tofu and chop it into cubes before transferring it to a food processor.

2. Blend the tofu on high speed until creamy, about 2 to 3 minutes.

3. Place the chocolate chips in a microwave-safe bowl and microwave on medium-high heat at 20-second intervals, stirring after each interval.

4. When it has melted, stir the chocolate until it is smooth and then drizzle it into the food processor while it is running on low speed.

5. Blend for 2 minutes until well combined.

6. Place the cream cheese in the bowl of a stand mixer and beat until smooth.

7. Scrape down the sides and add the sour cream and powdered sugar.

8. Beat the mixture on medium-high speed for about 1 minute; then beat it into the chocolate-tofu mixture.

9. Spoon the mousse into dessert cups and chill for 30 minutes before serving.

Per Serving Calories 429; Total fat: 29g; Saturated fat: 15g; Total carbs: 33g; Fiber: 1g; Cholesterol: 61mg; Protein: 15g

Raspberry Chocolate Trifle

Serves 4

This raspberry chocolate trifle is the perfect blend of tart raspberry flavor and creamy milk chocolate pudding, all with a little graham-cracker crunch.

24 chocolate graham crackers

½ cup plus 1 teaspoon coconut oil, divided

¼ cup granulated sugar

One 14-ounce box firm tofu

¼ cup unsweetened cocoa powder

One 3.12-ounce box milk chocolate pudding mix

½ cup light sour cream

2 cups fresh raspberries

½ cup chocolate chips

1. Break up the chocolate graham crackers by hand and place them in the food processor.

2. Pulse until the graham crackers are finely crushed and then transfer them to a bowl.

3. Melt ½ cup coconut oil and stir it into the grahams along with the sugar. Set the mixture aside.

4. Place the tofu in a food processor and blend until smooth.

5. Blend in the cocoa powder, pudding mix, and sour cream.

6. Blend the mixture on high speed for 1 to 2 minutes until creamy and well combined.

7. Divide the graham cracker mixture between four dessert cups and top with alternating layers of chocolate pudding and fresh raspberries.

8. Combine the chocolate chips and remaining 1 teaspoon coconut oil in a microwave-safe bowl and melt on high heat at 5- to 8-second intervals.

9. Drizzle the melted chocolate over the trifles to serve.

Per Serving Calories 654; Total fat: 41g; Saturated fat: 29g; Total carbs: 66g; Fiber: 9g; Cholesterol: 13mg; Protein: 13g

Almond Thumbprint Cookies

Makes 10 to 12 cookies • Serving size = 1 cookie

These almond thumbprint cookies have the added bonus of being completely gluten-free—that makes them a great option for individuals with gluten intolerance or Celiac disease.

½ cup unsalted butter, at room temperature

¼ cup granulated sugar

1 teaspoon almond extract

1 cup gluten-free all-purpose flour

Pinch of salt

1 egg, beaten

½ cup chopped almonds

½ cup raspberry jam

1. Preheat oven to 350°F and line two cookie sheets with parchment paper.

2. Combine the butter and sugar in the bowl of a stand mixer and beat on medium speed for about 2 minutes until light and fluffy.

3. Scrape down the sides of the bowl and add the almond extract.

4. Beat on medium speed for 1 minute; then scrape down the sides of the bowl and add the flour and salt.

5. Continue to beat the mixture for 30 seconds and then scrape down the sides of the bowl and add the egg.

6. Beat for 30 seconds; wrap the dough in plastic and chill for 1 hour.

7. Shape the dough into 1-inch balls by hand and set them aside.

8. Sprinkle the chopped almonds on a baking sheet and roll the balls through the chopped almonds.

9. Use your thumb to make a shallow indentation in the center of each ball and spoon about ½ teaspoon raspberry jam into the indentation.

10. Arrange the cookies on the prepared baking sheets and bake for 12 to 14 minutes until lightly browned.

11. Cool on wire racks before serving.

Per Serving Calories 217; Total fat: 12g; Saturated fat: 6g; Total carbs: 25g; Fiber: 2g; Cholesterol: 41mg; Protein: 3g

Snickerdoodles

Makes about 16 cookies • Serving size = 1 cookie

Snickerdoodles are a Christmastime favorite, and this recipe is sure to put you in the holiday spirit.

1 cup unsalted butter, at room temperature

1½ cups plus 2 tablespoons granulated sugar, divided

3 cups all-purpose flour

1 teaspoon baking soda

¾ teaspoon salt

1 teaspoon cream of tartar

1 egg, beaten

1½ teaspoons almond extract

2 teaspoons ground cinnamon

1. Preheat oven to 400°F and line two baking sheets with parchment paper.

2. Combine the butter and 1½ cups sugar in the bowl of a stand mixer and beat on medium speed for about 2 minutes, until light and fluffy.

3. Scrape down the sides of the bowl and add the flour, baking soda, salt, and cream of tartar.

4. Beat on medium speed for 1 minute, and then scrape down the sides of the bowl and add the egg and almond extract.

5. Continue to beat the mixture for 30 seconds, then turn the dough out into a bowl.

6. Form the dough into 1-inch balls by hand and set them on the baking sheets.

7. Combine the ground cinnamon and remaining 2 tablespoons granulated sugar in a small bowl and roll the cookie balls in the mixture.

8. Arrange the balls on the baking sheets and flatten them slightly with the tines of a fork.

9. Bake for 8 to 10 minutes until lightly golden.

Per Serving Calories 269; Total fat: 12g; Saturated fat: 7g; Total carbs: 38g; Fiber: 1g; Cholesterol: 41mg; Protein: 3g

Marshmallow Rice Bars

Serves 9 to 12 • Serving size = 1 bar

These marshmallow rice bars are better than any you might find at the grocery store. Not only are they fresh and delicious, but because you make them yourself you can be sure they are free from artificial additives.

1 tablespoon unsalted butter

2 cups vegetarian mini marshmallows

6 cups brown rice cereal

1. Melt the butter in a large pot over medium heat.

2. Stir in the marshmallows and cook until they are melted, about 5 minutes.

3. Remove the pot from the heat and stir in the brown rice cereal.

4. Line a 9x13-inch baking pan with aluminum foil and spoon the cereal mixture into the pan.

5. Press the cereal mixture firmly into the pan with the back of a wooden spoon.

6. Allow to cool for 10 to 15 minutes before cutting into bars to serve.

Per Serving Calories 74; Total fat: 1g; Saturated fat: 1g; Total carbs: 15g; Fiber: 1g; Cholesterol: 3mg; Protein: 1g

Chocolate Raspberry Bars

Serves 12 to 16 • Serving size = 1 bar

These chocolate raspberry bars are a unique dessert that is surprisingly easy to make. Don't be afraid to experiment with different flavors of jam—you might even want to try making your own homemade jam for this dessert!

1½ cups all-purpose flour

1 cup brown sugar, packed

1 teaspoon baking powder

1 cup unsalted butter, at room temperature

1½ cups old-fashioned oats

½ cup shredded coconut, unsweetened

½ cup chopped walnuts

1½ cups raspberry jam or preserves

½ cup semisweet chocolate chips

1. Preheat oven to 350°F and lightly grease and flour a square glass baking dish.

2. Combine the flour, brown sugar, and baking powder in the bowl of a stand mixer and beat on medium speed until well combined.

3. Add the butter 1 or 2 tablespoons at a time with the mixer running, beating for 10 to 12 seconds between each addition.

4. Beat in the oats, coconut, and chopped walnuts.

5. Spoon about one-third of the mixture into the prepared pan and spread it evenly.

6. Top the mixture with the raspberry jam or preserves and sprinkle with chocolate chips.

7. Spoon the rest of the dough mixture on top and spread evenly.

8. Bake for 25 to 30 minutes until browned and bubbling.

9. Cool on a wire rack for 30 minutes and cut into bars.

Per Serving Calories 424; Total fat: 20g; Saturated fat: 13g; Total carbs: 60g; Fiber: 2g; Cholesterol: 41mg; Protein: 3g

Peanut Butter Rice Bars

Makes about 18 bars • Serving size = 1 bar

These peanut butter rice bars are chewy and chocolaty with just the right amount of smooth peanut butter flavor.

8 cups brown rice cereal

¼ cup ground flaxseed

2 tablespoons unsweetened cocoa powder

1 cup brown rice syrup

½ cup peanut butter

¾ teaspoon vanilla extract

1. Lightly grease a 9x13-inch glass baking dish with cooking spray and set aside.

2. Stir together the brown rice cereal, ground flaxseed, and cocoa powder in a mixing bowl.

3. Combine the brown rice syrup, peanut butter, and vanilla extract in a small pan over medium heat.

4. Heat the mixture, stirring occasionally, until smooth and melted, about 5 minutes.

5. Pour the melted syrup mixture into the bowl with the cereal and stir well until it is completely incorporated.

6. Press the cereal mixture into the greased baking dish and pat it down evenly by hand.

7. Cover and chill for 1 hour before cutting into 18 bars.

Per Serving Calories 137; Total fat: 5g; Saturated fat: 1g; Total carbs: 23g; Fiber: 2g; Cholesterol: 0mg; Protein: 4g

Peanut Butter Brownies

Serves 12 to 16 • Serving size = 1 brownie

Peanut butter and chocolate are two flavors that were simply meant to be together. These peanut butter brownies are proof of that fact—deliciously delectable and surprisingly easy to bake!

2 cups all-purpose flour

2 cups granulated sugar

¾ cup unsweetened cocoa powder

1 teaspoon baking powder

¾ teaspoon salt

1 cup warm water

1 cup coconut oil, melted

1 teaspoon vanilla extract

¼ cup smooth peanut butter

1. Preheat oven to 350°F and line a 9x13-inch baking pan with foil.

2. Combine the flour, sugar, cocoa powder, baking powder, and salt in the bowl of a stand mixer.

3. With the mixer running on low speed, pour in the water, coconut oil, and vanilla extract.

4. Beat on medium speed for about 1 minute until the mixture is well blended.

5. Pour the batter into the prepared pan.

6. Spoon the peanut butter into the batter in five even dollops, one in each corner and one in the center of the pan.

7. Use a butter knife to swirl the peanut butter through the batter.

8. Bake for 20 to 25 minutes until the center is set.

9. Cool on a wire rack for about 30 minutes, and then turn the brownies out onto a flat surface and cut into bars to serve.

Per Serving Calories 403; Total fat: 22g; Saturated fat: 17g; Total carbs: 53g; Fiber: 3g; Cholesterol: 0mg; Protein: 5g

Vegan Apple Crisp

Serves 8 to 10 • Serving size = about ¾ cup

Dried cranberries give this apple crisp a hint of tartness that offsets the sweetness of the apples. Try it out on your family without telling them what's in it. They may not be able to identify the secret ingredient, but they will certainly be glad it is there!

1¼ cups all-purpose flour, divided

¾ cup granulated sugar

2 cups old-fashioned oats

½ tablespoon ground cinnamon

1 cup dried cranberries

6 cups sweet apples, thinly sliced

½ cup brown sugar, packed

8 tablespoons unsalted butter, at room temperature

1. Preheat oven to 425°F.

2. Combine ¼ cup flour with the sugar, oats, cinnamon, and dried cranberries in a mixing bowl.

3. Add the sliced apples and stir well to combine.

4. In the bowl of a stand mixer, combine the remaining flour with the brown sugar on medium speed.

5. Leaving the mixer running, add the butter about 1 tablespoon at a time until a crumbly mixture forms.

6. Transfer the apple mixture into a 2-quart casserole dish and spoon the crumbly mixture over top.

7. Place the casserole dish on a baking sheet and cover with aluminum foil.

8. Bake for 40 minutes; then remove the foil and reduce the oven temperature to 350°F.

9. Bake for another 10 minutes until lightly browned; cool for 10 minutes before serving.

Per Serving Calories 457; Total fat: 13g; Saturated fat: 8g; Total carbs: 82g; Fiber: 4g; Cholesterol: 31mg; Protein: 6g

Gluten-Free Red Velvet Cupcakes

Makes about 24 cupcakes • Serving size = 1 cupcake

These gluten-free red velvet cupcakes are a show-stopper. You won't be able to decide which is better, the beautiful color this recipe produces or the flavor of the light and fluffy cupcakes themselves!

1¾ cups gluten-free all-purpose flour

¾ cup unsweetened cocoa powder

2 teaspoons baking soda

1 teaspoon baking powder

2 cups granulated sugar

2 cups skim milk, divided

½ cup coconut oil, melted

1 tablespoon distilled white vinegar

1 teaspoon vanilla extract

2 tablespoons all-natural red food coloring

2 eggs, beaten

Vegan cream cheese frosting, store-bought

1. Preheat oven to 350°F and line two standard muffin pans with paper liners.

2. Combine the flour, cocoa, baking soda, and baking powder in the bowl of a stand mixer.

3. Beat in the sugar.

4. In another bowl, whisk together the milk, coconut oil, vinegar, vanilla extract, and food coloring.

5. With the stand mixer running on low speed, pour in the milk mixture and beat for 30 seconds until smooth; then beat in the eggs.

6. Spoon the batter into the prepared pans, filling each cup with ¼ cup batter.

7. Bake the cupcakes for 18 to 20 minutes or until a knife inserted in the center comes out clean.

8. Cool in the pans for 30 minutes before frosting with cream cheese frosting.

Per Serving (does not include frosting) Calories 152; Total fat: 5g; Saturated fat: 4g; Total carbs: 26g; Fiber: 2g; Cholesterol: 14mg; Protein: 3g

Vanilla Bean Cupcakes

Makes 12 to 14 cupcakes • Serving size = 1 cupcake

Made with real vanilla, these vanilla bean cupcakes are like nothing you've ever tried before. Top them with your favorite frosting to make them truly irresistible.

1½ cups granulated sugar

1 cup coconut oil

2 teaspoons vanilla extract

2 tablespoons fresh lemon juice

1 tablespoon fresh lemon zest

3 cups unbleached cake flour

1 tablespoon baking powder

½ cup warm water

1½ tablespoons Ener-G Egg Replacer

1 cup skim milk

1 tablespoon distilled white vinegar

1 vanilla bean

1. Preheat oven to 350°F and line a standard muffin pan with paper liners.

2. Combine the sugar, coconut oil, vanilla extract, lemon juice, and lemon zest in the bowl of a stand mixer.

3. Beat on medium speed until well combined and then scrape down the sides of the bowl.

4. Beat again on high speed for 2 minutes until fluffy.

5. In a separate bowl, whisk together the flour and baking powder.

6. In yet another bowl, combine the warm water, egg replacer, skim milk, and vinegar.

7. Beat about ½ of the dry ingredients into the bowl of the stand mixer and beat in the wet ingredients.

8. Scrape down the sides of the bowl and beat in the remainder of the dry ingredients until smooth.

→

9. Beat on medium speed for 30 seconds.

10. Using a small sharp knife, carefully split the vanilla bean down the center lengthwise.

11. Scrape the small black seeds into the batter and stir well.

12. Spoon the batter into the prepared pan, filling each up about one-third full.

13. Bake for 20 to 25 minutes or until a knife inserted in the center comes out clean.

14. Cool in the pan for 10 minutes before turning out onto wire racks to cool.

Per Serving Calories 290; Total fat: 18g; Saturated fat: 16g; Total carbs: 33g; Fiber: 0g; Cholesterol: 0mg; Protein: 2g

Red Velvet Layer Cake

Serves 8 to 10

If you are looking for a dessert that looks as good as it tastes, this red velvet layer cake will get the job done. The deep red color of the cake contrasts beautifully with the white of the cream cheese frosting to give you a picture-perfect dessert to share.

1 cup granulated sugar

⅔ cup unsalted butter, at room temperature

2½ tablespoons unsweetened cocoa powder

¾ teaspoon salt

2 teaspoons baking soda

6 tablespoons warm water

3 large eggs, beaten

1½ cups skim milk

2 tablespoons distilled white vinegar

1 teaspoon vanilla extract

3 tablespoons all-natural red food coloring

3½ cups unbleached pastry flour

Vegan cream cheese frosting, store-bought

1. Preheat oven to 350°F. Lightly grease and flour two 9-inch round cake pans.

2. Beat together the sugar, butter, cocoa powder, salt, and baking soda in the bowl of a stand mixer for about 2 minutes.

3. Whisk in the warm water, eggs, and milk, along with the vinegar, vanilla extract, and food coloring.

4. Keep the stand mixer running on low speed until the batter is smooth, and then divide evenly between the two prepared pans.

5. Bake for 25 to 30 minutes until a knife inserted in the center comes out clean.

6. Cool in the pans for 10 minutes; turn out onto wire racks to cool completely before frosting with cream cheese frosting.

Per Serving (does not include frosting) Calories 327; Total fat: 18g; Saturated fat: 10g; Total carbs: 39g; Fiber: 2g; Cholesterol: 111mg; Protein: 6g

Vegan Carrot Cake

Serves 8 to 10

Carrot cake is a classic recipe loved particularly by vegetarians—
it has "carrot" in the name, after all. This particular recipe is both
vegetarian- and vegan-friendly!

2½ cups unbleached
pastry flour

2 cups granulated sugar

1¾ teaspoons
baking powder

1¼ teaspoons
baking soda

¾ teaspoon salt

1 tablespoon ground
cinnamon

¾ cup unsweetened
flaked coconut

1½ cups chopped
walnuts, divided

4 tablespoons
warm water

1 tablespoon ener-g
egg replacer

1 cup canola oil

1 cup unsweetened
applesauce

1 teaspoon vanilla extract

2 cups raw carrots,
shredded

Vegan cream cheese
frosting, store-bought

1. Preheat oven to 350°F. Lightly grease and
flour two round 9-inch cake pans.

2. Beat together the pastry flour, sugar, baking
powder, baking soda, salt, and ground
cinnamon using a stand mixer.

3. Add the coconut and ½ cup chopped walnuts
and blend well.

4. In a small bowl, whisk together the warm
water and egg replacer.

5. Beat in the canola oil, applesauce, and
vanilla extract; then beat in the egg replacer
mixture.

6. Fold in the shredded carrots.

7. Divide the batter evenly between the two
prepared pans and bake for 30 to 35 minutes,
or until a knife inserted in the center of the
cakes comes out clean.

8. Allow the cakes to cool for 10 minutes, then
turn out onto wire racks to cool completely
before frosting and topping with the remaining
chopped walnuts.

Per Serving (does not include frosting) Calories 589;
Total fat: 36g; Saturated fat: 5g; Total carbs: 61g; Fiber: 3g;
Cholesterol: 0mg; Protein: 3g

Spiced Pumpkin Cake

Serves 12 • Serving size = 1 square

This moist and flavorful spice cake is the perfect fall treat. The cake itself is bursting with pumpkin flavor, topped with a sweetened cream cheese frosting.

1 cup whole-wheat flour

1 cup all-purpose flour

1½ cups brown sugar, packed

1¾ teaspoons baking powder

1¼ teaspoons baking soda

½ teaspoon salt

½ tablespoon ground cinnamon

⅛ teaspoon ground nutmeg

½ cup canola oil

½ cup skim milk

1 teaspoon vanilla extract

15 ounces organic pumpkin purée

1 egg, beaten

Vegan cream cheese frosting, store-bought

1. Preheat oven to 350°F and lightly grease and flour a 9x13-inch baking pan.

2. Combine the dry ingredients in the bowl of a stand mixer and beat on medium speed for 15 seconds to combine.

3. Drizzle in the canola oil and skim milk; then add the vanilla extract and pumpkin purée.

4. Beat the mixture for 30 seconds on medium speed and then scrape down the sides of the bowl.

5. Add the egg and beat for 30 seconds and then spoon the batter into the pan.

6. Bake for 25 to 30 minutes until a knife inserted in the center of the cake comes out clean.

7. Cool on a wire rack for 1 hour. Frost with vegan cream cheese frosting.

Per Serving (does not include frosting) Calories 280; Total fat: 10g; Saturated fat: 1g; Total carbs: 46g; Fiber: 3g; Cholesterol: 14mg; Protein: 4g

Pumpkin Roll

Serves 8 to 10 • Serving size = ½-inch slice

Pumpkin roll is a classic fall dessert that the whole family is sure to love. Serve it up with a glass of warm apple cider or hot cocoa on a cold winter night.

¾ cup all-purpose flour

1 cup granulated sugar

1 teaspoon baking soda

1 teaspoon ground cinnamon

2 eggs

⅔ cup organic pumpkin purée

3½ cups powdered sugar, divided

6 tablespoons unsalted butter, at room temperature

8 ounces cream cheese, at room temperature

1 teaspoon vanilla extract

1. Preheat oven to 350°F and lightly grease and flour a 10x15-inch rimmed baking sheet.

2. Combine the flour, sugar, baking soda, and cinnamon in the bowl of a stand mixer.

3. Add the eggs and pumpkin purée; beat on medium speed for 30 seconds until smooth.

4. Spread the batter in the prepared baking sheet and bake for 10 to 12 minutes, until a knife inserted into the center of the cake comes out clean.

5. Sprinkle a clean hand towel with about ½ cup powdered sugar.

6. Turn out the cake onto the towel and carefully roll it up; set aside to cool for 30 minutes.

7. Beat together the butter and cream cheese in the bowl of the stand mixer on medium speed for about 2 minutes until smooth.

8. Scrape down the sides of the bowl and then beat in the vanilla extract.

9. Leaving the mixer running, beat in the remaining 3 cups powdered sugar, about 1 cup at a time.

10. Whip the frosting on high speed for 1 minute.

11. Unroll the cake and spread the frosting evenly on top of it.

12. Carefully re-roll the cake using the towel and chill for 2 hours before slicing to serve.

Per Serving Calories 541; Total fat: 20g; Saturated fat: 12g; Total carbs: 89g; Fiber: 1g; Cholesterol: 95mg; Protein: 5g

Strawberry Cheesecake

Serves 12 to 16 • Serving size = 1 square

You can get all the delicious flavor of cheesecake with half the work by baking it in a rectangular pan rather than a springform pan. This strawberry cheesecake is cool and creamy, topped with just the right amount of strawberry flavor.

24 graham cracker squares

¼ cup unsalted butter, melted

1¾ cups granulated sugar, divided

Four 8-ounce packages cream cheese, at room temperature

4 eggs, beaten

1 cup strawberry jam

1 cup fresh strawberries, sliced

1. Preheat oven to 350°F and grease and flour a 9x13-inch baking pan.

2. Break the graham crackers up by hand into a food processor and blend until finely crushed.

3. Pour the graham crackers into a bowl and add the melted butter and ¼ cup granulated sugar.

4. Stir well to combine; pour the mixture into the prepared pan and press into the bottom and sides by hand.

5. Beat the cream cheese in the bowl of a stand mixer on medium speed for about 2 minutes.

6. Add the eggs and remaining 1½ cups sugar; beat until smooth.

7. Pour the mixture into the crust and bake for 40 to 45 minutes until the center is just set.

8. Chill overnight and then spread with strawberry jam and top with sliced strawberries.

9. Cut into bars to serve.

Per Serving Calories 593; Total fat: 33g; Saturated fat: 20g; Total carbs: 68g; Fiber: 1g; Cholesterol: 147mg; Protein: 9g

Conclusion

After reading this book you should have an understanding not only of what the vegetarian diet is, but what it can do for you. By eliminating meat from your diet, you can drastically reduce your risk for serious diseases, including type 2 diabetes, heart disease, and even cancer. Not only do you get the disease-fighting benefits of fruits and vegetables, but you get all of the other health benefits as well! After just a few weeks on a vegetarian diet you will notice that your skin is clearer, your hair shinier, and your nails stronger. You also shouldn't be surprised if you find that you seem to be bursting with energy and vitality!

As you've already learned, people switch to a vegetarian diet for different reasons. For some people, the motivation is purely medical or health related—they want to improve their diet to improve their health. For others, however, it is a matter of refusing to support the factory farming industry, which abuses animals and the environment. A switch to a vegetarian diet is a vote for sustainability and animal rights. Even if it seems unlikely that a single person removing meat from her diet would have a noticeable impact on the meat industry, just think about the awareness you can generate simply by sharing your choice with your family and friends.

Switching to a vegetarian diet is a personal choice and it is good for you. Do not let the skepticism of others set you back in your journey toward a healthier and happier you. By using the information you learned in reading this book, as well as the recipes provided, you are now ready to set out on a new adventure—the vegetarian lifestyle!

Glossary

Albumin a globular protein found in milk and eggs; often used in cosmetics as a coagulating agent and in baked goods.

Antioxidants molecules that prevent other molecules from oxidizing; they protect cells from free radical damage, and may also help prevent cancer and other chronic diseases.

Atherosclerosis a condition characterized by the thickening of artery walls as a result of the accumulation of cholesterol and other fatty materials.

Blender an electrical appliance used to purée or emulsify foods; called a liquidizer in the UK.

Casein a type of protein found in milk; often used as an additive in cheeses, nondairy creamers, and cosmetics.

Dehydrator an appliance that uses heat and air flow to remove moisture from food.

Detoxification the removal of a harmful substance, such as a poison or toxin, or the effect of such (*Merriam-Webster's Dictionary*, 11th edition).

Flexitarian also known as semi-vegetarian; a person who follows a mostly vegetarian diet but sometimes consumes meat or fish.

Food processor a kitchen appliance that can be used to peel, chop, or purée foods.

Fruitarian an individual who consumes only fruit, nuts, and seeds, as well as plant matter that can be gathered without harming or killing the plant.

Gelatin a colorless, flavorless substance derived from animal by-products, often used as a thickener in candies and puddings; produced by boiling the skin, tendons, ligaments, and bones of slaughtered livestock in water.

Juicer a kitchen appliance that extracts the juice from fresh fruits and vegetables by various means; there are three types: centrifugal, mastication, and triturating.

Lacto-ovo-vegetarian a type of vegetarian who consumes eggs, milk, dairy, and other animal products, including honey.

Lactose a type of sugar derived from the glucose and galactose in milk.

Lacto-vegetarian a vegetarian who consumes milk and dairy products, but does not consume eggs.

Ovo-vegetarian a vegetarian who consumes eggs, but does not consume milk or other dairy products.

Pescatarian an individual who abstains from all meat except for fish and seafood.

Phytochemicals, or phytonutrients, are compounds that naturally occur in plants and have biological significance (i.e., antioxidants).

Raw vegan an individual who follows a vegan diet but does not consume any food that has been heated above 115°F.

Seitan a meat substitute made from wheat; an excellent source of vegetarian protein.

Tempeh a meat substitute made from fermented soy beans and rice; a good source of vegetarian protein and dietary fiber.

Tofu also called bean curd; made by coagulating soy milk and pressing the curd into blocks.

Vegan an individual who practices veganism; may also apply to foods that meet the standards of a vegan diet.

Veganism the practice of abstaining from the use and consumption of animal products.

Vegetarian an individual who abstains from the consumption of meat and seafood; some vegetarians still consume eggs, milk, and other dairy products.

Vegetarianism the practice of abstaining from the consumption of animal-derived meat.

Vegetarian Society a society founded in Manchester, England, in 1847 to support and represent vegetarians in the United Kingdom while also spreading the word about the vegetarian lifestyle.

References and Resources

Anderson, Kathleen. "Excess Iron and Brain Degeneration: The Little-Known Link." LEF.org: Live Extension Magazine, March 2012. http://www.lef.org/magazine/mag2012/mar2012_Excess-Iron-Brain-Degeneration_01.htm

Bartzokis, George, T. A. Tishler, E. P. Raven, P. H. Lu, and L. L. Altshuler. "Premenopausal Hysterectomy Is Associated with Increased Brain Ferritin Iron." *Neurobiological Aging* 33, no. 9 (September 2012): 1950–8. http://www.ncbi.nlm.nih.gov/pubmed/21925770

Dai, Q., A. R. Borenstein, Y. Wu, J.C. Jackson, and E. B. Larson."Fruit and Vegetable Juices and Alzheimer's Disease: The Kame Project." *American Journal of Medicine* 119, no. 9 (September 2012): 751–9. http://www.ncbi.nlm.nih.gov/pubmed/16945610

Murphy, Andrew J., Nora Bijl, Laurent Yvan-Charvet, Carrie B. Welch, Neha Bhagwat, Adili Reheman, Yiming Wang, James A. Shaw, Ross L. Levine, Heyu Ni, Alan R. Tall, and Nan Wang. "Cholesterol Efflux in Megakaryocyte Progenitors Suppresses Platelet Production and Thrombocytosis." *Nature Medicine* 19, no. 5 (2013): 586–94. http://www.nature.com/nm/journal/v19/n5/abs/nm.3150.html

National Academy of Sciences Institute of Medicine Food and Nutrition Board. "Dietary Reference Intakes (DRIs): Estimated Average Requirements." http://www.iom.edu/Activities/Nutrition/SummaryDRIs/~/media/Files/Activity%20Files/Nutrition/DRIs/5_Summary%20Table%20Tables%201-4.pdf

Nicholson, A, and J. L. Howard. "The Medical Costs Attributable to Meat Consumption." *Preventive Medicine* 24 (1995): 646–55.

Pan, An, Qi Sun, Adam M. Bernstein, JoAnn E. Manson, Walter C. Willett, Frank B. Hu."Changes in Red Meat Consumption and Subsequent Risk of Type 2 Diabetes Mellitus." *The Journal of the American Medical Association Internal Medicine* 173, no. 14 (2013) http://archinte.jamanetwork.com/article.aspx?articleid=1697785

Pan, An, Q. Sun, A. M. Bernstein, M. B. Schulze, J. E. Manson, M. J. Stampfer, W. C. Willett, and F. B. Hu. "Red Meat Consumption and Mortality: Results from 2 Prospective Cohort Studies." *The Archives of Internal Medicine* 172, no. 7 (2012): 555–63. http://www.ncbi.nlm.nih.gov/pubmed/22412075>

Physicians Committee for Responsible Medicine (PCRM). "Meat Consumption and Cancer Risk." http://pcrm.org/search/?cid=3542

Rouse, I. L., B. K. Armstrong, and L. J. Beilin. "Vegetarian Diet, Lifestyle, and Blood Pressure in Two Religious Populations." *Journal of Clinical and Experimental Pharmacology and Physiology* 9, no. 3 (1982): 327–30. http://www.ncbi.nlm. nih.gov /pubmed/7140012

Sellmeyer, Deborah E., Katie L. Stone, Anthony Sebastian, Steven R. Cummings, and for the Study of Osteoporotic Fractures Research Group. "A High Ratio of Dietary Animal to Vegetable Protein Increases the Rate of Bone Loss and the Risk of Fracture in Postmenopausal Women." *The American Journal of Clinical Nutrition* 73, no. 1 (2001): 118–22. http://ajcn.nutrition.org/content/ 73/1/118.full

Tantamango-Bartley, Y., K. Jaceldo-Siegl, J. Fan, and G. Fraser. "Vegetarian Diets and the Incidence of Cancer in a Low-Risk Population." *Cancer Epidemiology Biomarkers and Prevention* 22, no. 2 (2013): 286–94. http://www.ncbi.nlm.nih .gov/pubmed/23169929

Tucker, K. L., M.T. Hannan, and D.P. Kiel. "The Acid-Base Hypothesis: Diet and Bone in the Framingham Osteoporosis Study." *European Journal of Nutrition* 40, no. 5 (2001): 231–7. http://www.ncbi.nlm.nih.gov/pubmed/11842948

Vegetarian Society. "History of the Vegetarian Society." https://www.vegsoc .org/history

Wang, Y., and M. A. Beydoun. "Meat Consumption is Associated with Obesity and Central Obesity among US Adults." *International Journal of Obesity* 33, no. 6 (2009): 621–8. http://www.ncbi.nlm.nih.gov/pubmed/19308071

World Cancer Research Fund/American Institute for Cancer Research. "Food, Nutrition, Physical Activity, and the Prevention of Cancer: A Global Perspective." Washington, DC: AICR (2007). http://eprints.ucl.ac.uk/4841/1/4841.pdf

Index of Recipes

Index

CPSIA information can be obtained
at www.ICGtesting.com
Printed in the USA
JSHW020707110122
21937JS00011B/128